Taming the Wild Horse of Shadow Education

Zhang analyses the phenomenon of private supplementary tutoring from a global perspective. The expansion of such tutoring alongside schooling is among the striking global shifts since the turn of the century. In many countries over half of the relevant cohorts of children receive private tutoring, with that proportion in some locations exceeding 80%. The sector has far-reaching implications for social inequalities, (in)efficiencies in educational processes, study burdens on students, family finances, innovation, and employment. Yet greatly-needed government regulations have typically been slow to catch up with the phenomenon.

Commentary in the volume juxtaposes countries with strong regulations with counterparts having weak regulations. Conceptually, the book considers forces changing the roles of multiple stakeholders, including governments, entrepreneurs, teachers, families and students.

A useful read for students and researchers interested in comparative education and governance.

Wei Zhang is a Professor in the Institute of Curriculum and Instruction (ICI) of East China Normal University (ECNU), Shanghai, and the Executive Director of the Centre for International Research in Supplementary Tutoring (CIRIST). She is a member of China's Ministry of Education expert committee on private tutoring, and director of the expert committee on materials for tutoring and lifelong education in the Shanghai Municipal Education Commission. She is also an Honorary Professor at Aarhus University in Denmark. In 2020 she was a Fellow in UNESCO's Global Education Monitoring Report team. She obtained her doctorate from the University of Hong Kong, where she subsequently managed its Comparative Education Research Centre (CERC). She has published extensively in the domain of shadow education from an international comparative perspective, and has conducted fieldwork on the theme in Cambodia, Denmark, Mainland China, Hong Kong, Japan, and Myanmar.

Taming the Wild Horse of Shadow Education
The Global Expansion of Private Tutoring and Regulatory Responses

Wei Zhang

LONDON AND NEW YORK

First published 2023
by Routledge
4 Park Square, Milton Park, Abingdon, Oxon OX14 4RN

and by Routledge
605 Third Avenue, New York, NY 10158

Routledge is an imprint of the Taylor & Francis Group, an informa business

© 2023 Wei Zhang

The right of Wei Zhang to be identified as author of this work has been asserted in accordance with sections 77 and 78 of the Copyright, Designs and Patents Act 1988.

The Open Access version of this book, available at www.taylorfrancis.com, has been made available under a Creative Commons Attribution-Non Commercial-No Derivatives 4.0 license.

Trademark notice: Product or corporate names may be trademarks or registered trademarks, and are used only for identification and explanation without intent to infringe.

British Library Cataloguing in Publication Data
A catalogue record for this book is available from the British Library

ISBN: 978-1-032-33155-3 (hbk)
ISBN: 978-1-032-33156-0 (pbk)
ISBN: 978-1-003-31845-3 (ebk)

DOI: 10.4324/9781003318453

Typeset in Times
by KnowledgeWorks Global Ltd.

Author's notes

This book was produced in collaboration with the Centre for International Research in Supplementary Tutoring (CIRIST), East China Normal University (ECNU), Shanghai and the UNESCO Chair in Comparative Education at the University of Hong Kong (HKU).

The designations employed and the presentation of material throughout this publication do not imply the expression of any opinion whatsoever on the part of the publishers, CIRIST, ECNU, HKU or UNESCO concerning the legal status of any country, territory, city or area or of its authorities, or the delimitation of its frontiers and boundaries.

The author is responsible for the choice and the presentation of the facts in this book and for the opinions expressed therein, which are not necessarily those of the above-named bodies.

Contents

Illustrations ix
List of Boxes x
List of Abbreviations xi
Executive Summary xiii
Foreword by Mark Bray xvi

Introduction 1

PART I
A Global Framework 5

  1 Conceptual Framework 7
  2 What Needs to Be Regulated, Why and How? 15

PART II
Five Country Studies 43

  3 Japan: Changing Dynamics of Regulation and Self-Regulation 45
  4 China: Strong State Confronting Strong Market 58
  5 India: Diversity in a Decentralised System 79
  6 Egypt: Teachers as Tutors 89
  7 Denmark: Students as Tutors 97

PART III
Conclusions 107

8 Learning from Comparing 109

Appendix 121
References 128
Index 150

Illustrations

Figures

1.1	Understanding the Diversity of Shadow Education	8
1.2	Themes and Links for Comparative Analysis of Laws and Regulations for Shadow Education	13
3.1	Expansion of Gakushu Juku, 1981–2018, Japan	46
3.2	Changing Gakushu Juku Enrolment Rates by Level of Schooling, 1976–2007, Japan	46
3.3	Juku Self-Regulation and Public-Private Partnerships in Japan	56
8.1	An Expanded Conceptual Framework for Regulating Shadow Education	117

Tables

2.1	Curfews on Tutoring Companies in South Korea, by Location and Level of Education	25
3.1	Juku Expansion and Evolution, Japan, Post-WWII to the 1990s	48
5.1	Enrolment Rates in Private Tutoring, by Level of Education, India, 2017/18 (%)	81
5.2	Enrolment Rates in Private Tutoring, by State/Union Territory, India, 2017/18 (%)	81
8.1	Categories of Shadow Education Policy	114

Boxes

2.1	What about the effectiveness of private tutoring?	18
2.2	Violations of Japan's Act against Unjustifiable Premiums and Misleading Representations	24
2.3	What attracts teachers to tutoring?	29
3.1	Egalitarian rhetoric, meritocratic schooling and hierarchical society – the need for "double schooling"	50
4.1	Side-effects from the dynamic blacklists and whitelists	67
4.2	Educational commitments marginalised by advertisement arms race, and educational goals marginalised by pursuit of profits	68
5.1	Parental dismay at tutoring prohibition in Tripura State, India	83
5.2	Coaching centres in India – A case for regulation	85
6.1	Peer pressure, social competition and prestige	92

List of Abbreviations

AI	Artificial Intelligence
ARP	American Rescue Plan
ASP	After-School Programme
AUD	Australian dollar
CAA	Consumer Affairs Agency
CEO	Chief Executive Officer
CIRIST	Centre for International Research in Supplementary Tutoring
CFPS	China Family Panel Studies
CSR	Corporate Social Responsibility
ECNU	East China Normal University
EBS	Educational Broadcasting System
EEF	Education Endowment Foundation
EFA	Education for All
ESSA	Every Child Succeeds Act
GDP	Gross Domestic Product
GEM Report	Global Education Monitoring Report
GOSC	General Office of the State Council
GPA	Grade Point Average
ICI	Institute of Curriculum and Instruction
JJA	Japan Juku Association
MDG	Millennium Development Goal
METI	Ministry of Economy, Trade and Industry
MEXT	Ministry of Education, Culture, Sports, Science and Technology
MHLW	Ministry of Health, Labour & Welfare
MITI	Ministry of International Trade and Industry
MoE	Ministry of Education
MOSA	Ministry of Social Affairs
NCLB	No Child Left Behind

NCRHC	National Criminal Record History Check
NDRC	National Development and Reform Commission
NGO	Non-Governmental Organisation
NIRA	National Institute for Research Advancement
NPO	Non-Profit Organisation
NPSS	National Partnership for Student Success
NTP	National Tutoring Programme
OECD	Organisation for Economic Co-operation and Development
PISA	Programme for International Student Assessment
PPP	Public-Private Partnership
RTE	Right to Education
SACMEQ	Southern and Eastern Africa Consortium for Measuring Educational Quality
SAMR	State Administration for Market Regulation
SDG	Sustainable Development Goal
SEC	State Education Commission
SES	Supplemental Education Services
SMEC	Shanghai Municipal Education Commission
STA	Shanghai Tutoring Association
UNESCO	United Nations Educational, Scientific and Cultural Organization
USA	United States of America
WWCC	Working with Children Check
WWII	World War II

Executive Summary

Recent decades have brought huge expansion of private supplementary tutoring. This tutoring has far-reaching implications for social and economic development, and has a backwash on mainstream schooling. The tutoring sector has developed vigorously, and with relatively little government control. As such, it can be viewed as a wild horse in need of harnessing. This book addresses ways in which this can, and to some extent has been, done. It draws on comparative analysis from a wide range of contexts, first highlighting the need for regulation and then examining potential strategies.

Beginning with geography, during the second half of the 20th-century private supplementary tutoring was especially associated with parts of East Asia, particularly Japan and South Korea. It was also evident in parts of Europe, the Middle East and South Asia, but in these regions it received less attention. Now it has become a truly global phenomenon, evident for example even in the Scandinavian countries that had previously seemed to have top-quality school systems that did not need supplementation.

In the academic literature, private supplementary tutoring is widely called shadow education. The metaphor is used because much of its content mimics that in schooling: as the curriculum changes in the schools, so it changes in the shadow. In line with much of the literature, the present study focuses on supplementary tutoring provided on a fee-charging basis at the levels of primary and secondary education. It concerns a range of providers, among which individuals and entrepreneurs running corporate enterprises are the most important. Among the individuals are regular teachers in public schools who undertake tutoring on a part-time basis. This tutoring may be provided one-to-one, in small groups or in large classes. Most tutoring is provided in a face-to-face mode, but online tutoring has become increasingly important and is likely to expand further.

xiv *Executive Summary*

Although almost all governments around the world have regulations in place for both public and private schooling, regulations for private supplementary tutoring are much less evident. This book presents a conceptual framework that identifies definitions and parameters, stresses the need to think beyond conventions in the school sector, and notes market dynamics in distinct settings of shadow education. It then presents a five-dimensional model for regulating shadow education, placing laws and regulations in the centre and then considering deployment of the necessary personnel, partnerships of various kinds, self-regulation by tutoring providers, and empowerment of consumers.

Turning specifically to what needs to be regulated, why and how, the book stresses urgency evidenced not only by surges in the scale of private tutoring but also by the likelihood of much further expansion. Regulations, the book argues, are needed for social protection in an otherwise potentially exploitative environment. Considerations then address regulations first for companies that provide tutoring and second for supplementary tutoring provided by serving teachers in schools. In some settings, public-private partnerships demand consideration.

To complement the wide range of countries from which examples are drawn in the preceding chapters, the next chapter presents case studies of Japan, China, India, Egypt and Denmark. Japan has a long history of private tutoring, aspects of which have been regulated by the Ministry of Economy, Trade and Industry (METI), but with little involvement of the Ministry of Education, Culture, Sports, Science & Technology (MEXT). Yet in recent years, MEXT at the national level and counterparts at the sub-national levels have taken more active roles. The Chinese authorities have also taken active roles, particularly with leadership from the national level. They have found, however, that enactment of regulations may be challenging in ways that had not been anticipated. India provides an instructive contrast from a lower-income setting with a federal system and much internal diversity. Egypt also has a long history of shadow education and corresponding government efforts at control that have had limited success. Finally, the focus on Denmark brings a completely different context from a Scandinavian country with a strong public education system that has nevertheless seen emergence of shadow education in recent years.

The next chapter draws threads together to highlight lessons from experience. It commences with a summary of commonalities but also some diversities in aspirations, mandates and goals, and then remarks

Executive Summary xv

on challenges and successes in moving from vision to enactment. The constraints are mentioned so that planners and policy-makers can play their roles with circumspection and pragmatism.

Concluding, the book again observes that much more attention is needed to the regulation of tutoring by different types of providers and in different modes, with the goal of harnessing the strengths of non-state actors to serve the common good. Four core messages are identified, namely:

- shadow education is here to stay, so it is best to regulate it before too late;
- policies for shadow education should encompass multiple reference points;
- shadow education and schooling must be considered together; and
- partnerships should go beyond the modes of commercial trade.

The book shows the value of comparative analysis to identify not only the objectives but also the strategies to achieve them.

Foreword
Mark Bray[1]

I have much pleasure in writing the Foreword to this insightful, comprehensive and globally comparative work. It brings a considerable advance in the field, and will be of great value to both academics and policy makers.

As explained in the Introduction, the origin of the book lies in a Background Paper for UNESCO's Global Education Monitoring (GEM) Report. That report focused on the roles of non-state actors in education, recognising that teachers and companies that provide private supplementary tutoring are among significant but often-overlooked actors (UNESCO, 2021). Zhang's Background Paper, focusing on regulations for private tutoring, was a crucial ingredient and has been revised and elaborated in the book that you are now reading. The Background Paper was prepared following Zhang's appointment in 2020 to a prestigious GEM Fellowship.

Further setting the scene for this Foreword, I have myself long-standing relationships with UNESCO and almost equally long-standing focus on private tutoring, again with publications for both academics and policy makers. During the two decades from the mid-1980s, I undertook multiple assignments for UNESCO in Africa, Asia and Europe, some of which caused me to look closely at shadow education. My first book on the theme was published by UNESCO's International Institute for Educational Planning (IIEP) in 1999, and followed by a second in 2003 (Bray, 1999, 2003). Since 1986, I had been employed by the University of Hong Kong (HKU), but in 2006 I was granted leave to work for four years in Paris as the IIEP Director. That period included a Policy Forum on the shadow education which led to a further book (Bray, 2009), now available in 21 languages.

Returning to HKU in 2010, I received within months an application from Zhang Wei to study for a PhD with a focus on shadow education under my supervision. Her application showed much talent and vision. She held a first degree in Russian with a minor in Japanese from Peking University – usually considered the top university in China – and a research master's degree from the University of Oslo in Norway. She had already thought carefully not only about shadow education as an object of research but also about methods for researching it. Following arrival, she worked with great commitment and perceptiveness over three years to produce an excellent doctoral thesis about shadow education in one Chinese municipality (Zhang, 2013). She also engaged in various side projects, including research on shadow education in Hong Kong and an internship in Bangkok at UNESCO's Asia and Pacific Regional Bureau for Education.

Following her graduation, Zhang Wei remained at HKU to work as a post-doctoral fellow and Secretary of the Comparative Education Research Centre (CERC) of which I was the Director. She published work from her thesis and other projects, broadening her horizons with empirical research on shadow education in Cambodia, Myanmar and Japan. She also assisted with CERC projects that included a Policy Forum on the IIEP model, leading to a book about regulations for private tutoring in Asia (Bray & Kwo, 2014). She subsequently led a 2017 Policy Forum on public-private partnerships in shadow education.

In 2018, Zhang Wei moved from Hong Kong to a prestigious professorship at East China Normal University (ECNU), Shanghai. It was a special scheme for applicants under the age of 35, and again showed recognition of her talent, diligence and leadership abilities. I had by that time reached the official retirement age at HKU, and found myself responding to a different level of ECNU recruitment as a Distinguished Chair Professor while simultaneously retaining the UNESCO Chair in Comparative Education in HKU. The ECNU authorities recognised the significance of shadow education, and in 2019 established the Centre for International Research in Supplementary Tutoring (CIRIST) as the world's first research centre devoted specifically to this theme.

In recent years, major government-directed transformations have been evident in China's shadow education sector. Most obvious among milestones have been policies announced in 2018 and 2021 and with far-reaching impact (China, 2018, 2021). Because of her professional links and recognition, Zhang Wei was consulted not only by the government at different levels but also by the tutoring industry in dimensions of formulation and enactment of these policies. Her role and impact were evident not only at the national level but also in Shanghai which, as China's largest city with much administrative and entrepreneurial talent, was characterised by strong sub-national leadership.

Equally, Zhang Wei has wide international links facilitated by her linguistic abilities and professional networks. Thus the chapter on Japan in this book draws on her links with policy makers, entrepreneurs and researchers in that country. She has collaborated for example with the Japan Juku Association as well as with tutorial enterprises and government personnel. On the other side of world, in 2019 she engaged in extended fieldwork in Denmark, and in 2020 she was appointed an Honorary Professor of Aarhus University. Alongside, Zhang Wei has multiple professional links in other countries, including India and Egypt which are the foci of other chapters. Some of these links have been secured through UNESCO, but others reflect her parallel networks through academic circles and beyond.

In summary, this book draws on work stretching for over a decade and touching all corners of the globe. The earlier version released by the GEM Report team has already had significant impact, and this elaborated version with updated commentary, enlarged scope and enhanced conceptualisation takes the work further. The book is a milestone in the development of the field of shadow education – and I have every confidence that much more will follow in Zhang Wei's continuing career trajectory.

Note

1 Distinguished Chair Professor and Director of the Centre for International Research in Supplementary Tutoring (CIRIST), East China Normal University; and UNESCO Chair Professor in Comparative Education, The University of Hong Kong.

Introduction

Private supplementary tutoring probably has a history as long as that of schooling itself. For decades and even centuries, it has been a mechanism through which parents have sought to support and enhance their children's school performance, particularly in academic subjects. Until relatively recent times, however, it has been very modest in scale and mostly restricted to upper-class families.

In most countries, the significant changes came towards the end of the 20th century and/or beginning of the 21st century. Initially, private supplementary tutoring became strongly visible in East and South Asia (Bray, 1999). Then, since the turn of the century, it became visible in all other world regions and is now a global phenomenon (Bray, 2017; Entrich, 2020; Hajar & Karakus, 2022). This tutoring can play many positive roles, most obviously that it contributes to learning and to child socialisation, and it also provides employment and tax revenues. The tutoring also provides employment for tutors and associated support services. However, it also demands substantial household expenditures and both maintains and exacerbates social inequalities.

The dramatic expansion of supplementary tutoring around the world, mostly reflecting self-interested entrepreneurship by tutoring providers rather than wider social goals, underlies the "wild horse" metaphor in the title of this book. Many governments felt that their responsibilities were for schooling and that private tutoring could be left to the marketplace beyond the remit of Ministries of Education. Yet experience has shown that private tutoring can have far-reaching implications and that it is desirable for the horse at least to be harnessed and perhaps to be tamed. The ways to do this vary according to wider cultures and structures of government. Such matters are the focus of this book.

Private supplementary tutoring is commonly known as shadow education because much of its content mimics that in mainstream

DOI: 10.4324/9781003318453-1

schools: as the curriculum changes in the mainstream, so it changes in the shadow (Bray, 1999, 2009; Zhang & Yamato, 2018). While the metaphor of the shadow has limitations, it is nevertheless useful and in this book will be employed interchangeably with private [supplementary] tutoring.

The origins of the book lie in a Working Paper for UNESCO's Global Education Monitoring (GEM) Report. These reports focus on progress in education towards the Sustainable Development Goals, and particularly the fourth goal (SDG4), approved by the United Nations in 2015. This goal is to "Ensure inclusive and equitable quality education and promote lifelong learning opportunities for all" by 2030 (UNESCO, 2017a). Yet many commentators are aware that if left to market forces, various forms of private education are likely to be *ex*clusive and *in*equitable and thus to pull in the opposite direction to SDG4.

With such matters in mind, the GEM Report leadership decided that the 2021/2 issue of the report would focus on the roles of non-state actors in education (UNESCO, 2021a). Most obvious among these actors are operators of private schools. However, the Concept Note for the report (UNESCO, 2019, p. 6) appropriately recognised a much broader spread of actors, including providers of private supplementary tutoring. The Concept Note rightly observed (p. 6) that this widespread phenomenon "is often overlooked in analyses of non-state activity in education". This study helps to remedy that neglect.

Focusing particularly on regulations, this book draws on a wide array of written materials in multiple languages. Chief among these materials are the regulations themselves and commentaries on both the content and the implementation (or non-implementation) in the academic literature, newspapers and websites. The report also draws on the author's interviews, observations, case studies, and related professional interactions with personnel in tutorial companies, governments and professional associations at national and subnational levels, families and schools in China, Japan, the Republic of Korea, the USA, Denmark, Cambodia, and Myanmar. The study further draws on the author's surveys of parents, students and teachers in China, and on dialogues with colleagues who have conducted parallel work in other contexts.

The study is based on a combination of existing literature and the author's independent conceptual work. It aims to assist the readers to distinguish tutoring from schooling, in order to extend their understanding of policies. Three decades of shadow education research have shown many dimensions that ought to be taken into consideration in policy-making and implementation, but policy makers do not always think in such frameworks. Thus, analysis shows that some regulations do reflect an awareness of the nature and diversity of shadow education, for instance considering seasonal changes and categories of providers; but some dimensions are mostly neglected.

Thus, among the major thrusts of this analysis is first what the regulations (do not) say, and second how they have (not) been enacted. Even a cursory review shows that regulations are commonly ignored, which raises questions about their purpose that require attention. With one of the foci of SDG4 in mind, the study is especially interested in matters of social equity. The author also has a particular interest in regulations on innovative tools for teaching and learning, including the nature and uses of technology. Issues of moving targets also require consideration. Regulatory systems are commonly slow to keep up with reality, and even schools do not always know how to handle technology in ways that have sufficient safeguards e.g. of privacy.

With such matters in mind, Part I presents a conceptual framework that explains the definitions and nature of private supplementary tutoring, the market dynamics in different settings and the types of regulations considered. Specifically, two chapters focus first on what needs to be regulated and why, and second on who needs to be regulated and how. The latter section has two main foci, namely companies that provide tutoring and teachers in mainstream schools who provide private tutoring in addition to their main occupations. Part II then focuses on five country studies. Three are in Asia (Japan, China and India), one is in North Africa (Egypt), and the last is in Europe (Denmark). This provides a wide range of governance styles, income groups and educational traditions from which to draw comparative insights. Then Part III summarises lessons from failures and successes in regulations across the globe, before wrapping up in conclusion.

Part I
A Global Framework

1 Conceptual Framework

1.1 Definitions and parameters

Beginning with the concept of private supplementary tutoring, the discussion in this book is guided by the definition provided by Bray (1999) which has also been followed in many other studies (e.g. Aslam & Atherton, 2014; Zhang & Yamato, 2018; Luo & Chan, 2022). This definition has three main components:

- *Supplementation*. The focus is on subjects that are already covered in school, providing repetition and/or elaboration of the content.
- *Privateness*. The focus is on tutoring provided in exchange for a fee. It does not include free tutoring e.g. by relatives or by teachers as part of their school duties.
- *Academic*. The focus is on academic subjects, particularly examinable ones such as languages, mathematics and sciences. It does not include music or sport learned mainly for more rounded personal development.

Concerning levels of education, the study focuses on primary and secondary schooling. Private supplementary tutoring does also exist at pre-primary and post-secondary levels, but they are excluded in order to permit greater depth of analysis.

The word "tutoring" should also be explained. Sometimes this word is taken to imply one-to-one instruction. This type of activity is certainly included, but so are activities in small groups, full classes and even large lecture theatres. Further, much private supplementary tutoring is now provided over the internet as well as face-to-face. Figure 1.1 illustrates diverse modes of shadow education (viewed as a synonym for private supplementary tutoring) that may be considered. It includes hybrid models such as the dual-tutor mode which blends

DOI: 10.4324/9781003318453-3

8 A Global Framework

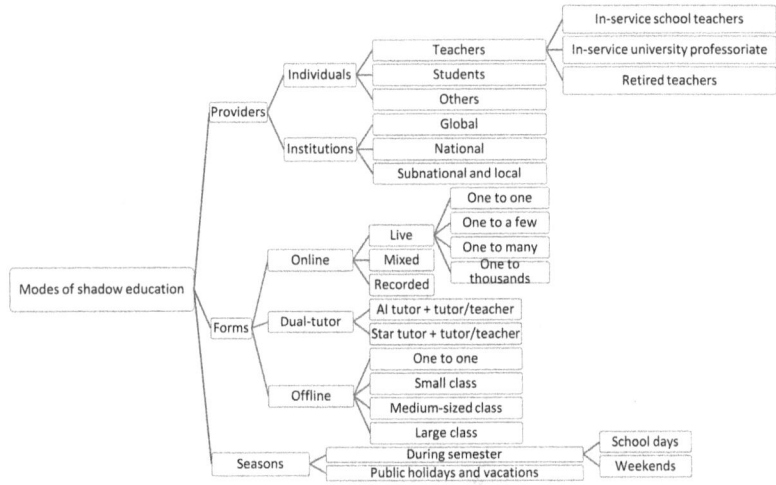

Figure 1.1 Understanding the Diversity of Shadow Education
Source: Zhang & Bray (2020, p. 328).

online and offline tutoring. Dual tutoring employs live tutors or artificial intelligence (AI) tutors operating through the internet in conjunction with teaching assistants in classrooms many kilometres away.

1.2 Thinking beyond the box of schooling

Unlike formal schooling, which is relatively standardised, uniform, stable and slow in change, private tutoring is diverse, fluid and adaptive to change. Thus, standard assumptions about effective regulations in schooling may not apply to shadow education. Regulations that neglect the diversity and fluidity of shadow education may be counterproductive in implementation.

Different providers, forms and seasons of tutoring have different implications for policy and practice. The Introduction mentioned that much of the present study is concerned with companies and with regular school teachers who provide private tutoring as an extra activity. Other providers include university students seeking pocket money, retirees and various other categories of people desiring extra incomes from informal or semi-formal work. Individuals in these groups may be self-employed or work for tutoring companies. The activities of self-employed tutors cannot easily be regulated in a top-down way, but empowerment of consumers can encourage such providers to engage in self-regulation and still be held accountable (Bray & Kwo, 2014, pp. 53–55). In-service teachers who provide supplementary tutoring may have their main employment in either public or private schools, with the latter in effect implying private plus more private provision.

Companies are the major institutional providers, but recent years have seen increasing involvement of non-profit organisations (NPOs), partly as a result of expanding publicly funded tutoring. Tutoring enterprises vary greatly in size. The smallest could be run by just one tutor without assistance, while the largest operates with franchises across the globe. Technological advances have also brought significant organisational changes. Tutoring through the internet no longer requires the tutors and tutees to be in the same location, and indeed they may not even be in the same country.

Large companies commonly find themselves under more pressure to comply with regulations since they attract more attention from both governments and consumers. Such companies are also more likely to have professional legal consultants to help interpret laws and regulations for both compliance and circumvention. Transnational, national and sub-national companies operating across geographical boundaries devise institutional policies according to the government policies of jurisdictions in which they operate. To regulate such companies, governments can benefit from partnerships across jurisdictions, especially in precautions against child abuse, privacy infringement and business failure.

Further diversity is evident not only in modes of tutoring but also in locations. It can take place at home, in classrooms, in public libraries and in cafés as well as via the internet. One-to-one and small-group tutoring in private venues make tutees more vulnerable to tutors and to issues of inappropriate sexual or other behaviour. Online live tutoring also brings risks of exposing children to sexual and violent content and is especially difficult to trace and regulate. However, some authorities are catching up with these matters. The Chinese government, for instance, has established national and local online systems for registration, supervision and information disclosure; and for self-regulation, the largest company has devised a monitoring system using AI to oversee tutor and tutee behaviour and to report problematic content online (Tomorrow Advancing Life, 2020).

The schedules for tutoring are the reverse of those of schooling, i.e. the shadow sector is quiet when the schools are in session and is active when the schools are out of session. Scheduling variations have implications not only for the venues of tutoring but also for the deployment of personnel in policy enforcement. Concerning venues, Cambodia and Mauritius are among the countries in which school premises are commonly used by teachers for private tutoring after official school hours. And concerning personnel deployment, inspectors in South Korea work late in the evenings to oversee tutoring centres' compliance with curfew regulations.

1.3 Market dynamics in the distinct settings of shadow education

The market dynamics of shadow education activities vary according to the contexts, but some general patterns can be observed. Generally, shadow education is provided in three types of settings, with different implications for emphases and foci of regulations:

1 a market *dominated by teachers*, in which teachers and perhaps schools are heavily involved in tutoring, e.g. Cambodia, Egypt, Ghana, Turkey and Uzbekistan;
2 a market *dominated by tutoring enterprises*, in which the industry is professionalised and tutoring enterprises are the major players (usually with strong and aggressive leading companies), e.g. Australia, Canada, France, Japan, South Korea, and the USA; and
3 a *mix* of the two previous categories, e.g. United Arab Emirates.

Concerning the first setting, different forms of involvement can be categorised as follows:

- teachers/schools providing tutoring (teachers as tutors);
- teachers/schools running tutoring enterprises (teachers as managers/owners);
- teachers obtaining commissions through referrals (teachers as brokers);
- teachers providing packaged services in the form of "home stay", in which the tutees live and eat at the teachers' homes under their supervision and receive tutoring in flexible schedules (teachers as tutors and child-carers).

These models are most evident in societies where mainstream schooling rushed into universal compulsory education despite lacking necessary financial and human resources, and/or where the teachers' salaries (as well as status in some settings) are low. The inadequate purchasing power of teachers' salaries is frequently cited by teachers as the main reason for involvement in tutoring. However, as evidenced in China, once the practice has become normalised in a society, the phenomenon is unlikely to go away even when salaries rise. In situations of resource constraint, not only do teachers perceive a need to offer tutoring for income to support their families, but some schools also consider tutoring a strategy to maintain student performance and operations. Even some policy makers have vested interests in tutoring, given great challenges in financing and other support. In resource-constrained settings, moreover, commercial tutoring companies and other tutoring providers are usually absent or limited in scale. Yet disparate patterns can be observed at subnational levels. For instance, research in settings as different as Cambodia and The Gambia has shown that compared to the capital city, where tutoring companies and college students are relatively accessible, tutoring in rural areas and less developed regions is mainly supplied by school teachers and to some extent schools.

In the second setting, formal schooling is better resourced and teachers' salaries are relatively high. Teachers therefore enjoy good welfare, job security and social status, and have less need to provide tutoring. Schools and governments also have less incentive to permit or encourage tutoring to cover potential deficits in financial and human resources at the institutional and system levels. Further, in settings like Hong Kong (China) and Japan, teachers are so busy with schoolwork that they have little time or energy for tutoring. Their counterparts in Sweden and Norway may have more time, but do not feel comfortable with the idea of private tutoring alongside their public responsibilities.

Elsewhere, however, dynamics may differ. For example in England and Wales, teachers have increasingly offered private tutoring as a way to earn extra incomes and, in some cases, secure professional satisfaction that they felt was more difficult to secure in the increasingly bureaucratised public school system. A 2019 survey of 1,678 teachers conducted on behalf of the Sutton Trust found that 24% of sampled secondary school teachers had provided private tutoring outside their schools during the previous two years (Sutton Trust, 2019). Two-thirds of the teachers who had tutored had done so after direct contact with parents, and others had tutored through agencies or NPOs.

The shifts in balances caused by the closure of schools during the COVID-19 pandemic deserve elaboration. As noted by Williamson and Hogan (2020), the rise of online tutoring was evident in multiple cultures. Further, in countries as different as the USA and Kenya, working parents in particular hired teachers to tutor their children (Daley, 2020; Asenath Maobe cited in Bray, 2021b, p. 63). Such arrangements might have been viewed as a short-term solution, but in many countries, it legitimated the practice and is likely to have lasting impact on both demand and supply.

1.4 A five-dimensional model for regulating shadow education

Turning to the matter of regulations, core questions concern the roles of the state and the market, their respective limitations, and their interactions and balances. Many governments have adopted a *laissez faire* approach to the tutoring sector (Bray, 2009, 2011; Bray & Kwo, 2014). Some that have woken up to the importance of regulating have found that the phenomenon has become too normalised, widespread and complicated for the policies to be readily effective. Japan presents a slightly different example of modest state interventions supplemented by strong self-regulation and consumer supervision. The marketplace has played a major role in regulating the industry and its professional development. Nevertheless, some participants and observers have frowned at the perceived price of institutionalisation of tutoring in the society, described as "the second schooling" for the private good. These stakeholders also frowned at the decades of market disorder as the industry expanded in the 1960s and 1970s. A few jurisdictions such as South Korea, Taiwan and Mainland China (since 2018) have been characterised by strong state interventions in regulation.

Policy embraces both text and processes, and its enactment rarely leads to simple answers about what is implementable and successful (Ball, 2006; Lingard & Ozga, 2009; Ball et al., 2012). Policy is non-linear, interactive and multidirectional (Lingard & Sellar, 2013). This general statement also applies in the specific domain of private supplementary tutoring (see e.g. Bray, 2009, 2011; Bray & Kwo, 2014; Zhang, 2019). The literature explores what works/fails in what contexts, to what extent, with whom and how, and shows that policy texts can send different messages to different actors according to their interpretations. Actors in the tutoring market are not merely passive subjects who implement policies or get implemented upon. Rather, they interpret and respond to the policies with varied capacities and agendas, and, even in the context of strong states, make active decisions in compliance, mediation or contestation (Ball et al., 2012). In addition to the tutoring suppliers who are the target to be regulated, families on the demand side are also key actors in the enactment processes.

Conceptual Framework 13

The above paragraphs are mainly concerned with government policies, but the principles can also apply to institutions. Thus, companies and schools providing tutoring have written and/or unwritten policies on ways to manage their operations, and professional associations may have written and/or unwritten policies for their members and the wider industry. This analysis can usefully embrace not only laws that could lead to legal action in courts in the case of infringement and regulations that have a softer framework and can be issued by Ministries of Education and comparable bodies rather than by parliaments and other legislatures, but also institutional policies of various kinds. All such analyses should be considered in their contexts, as depicted in Figure 1.2.

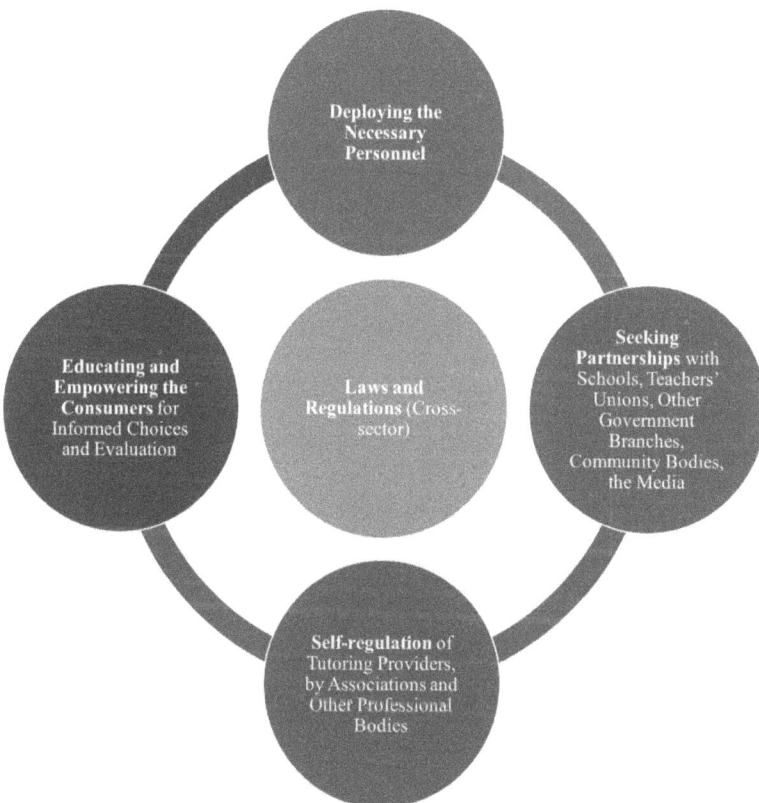

Figure 1.2 Themes and Links for Comparative Analysis of Laws and Regulations for Shadow Education

Source: Zhang & Bray (2020, p. 332).

Also needing recognition is that full enactment of laws and regulations requires the deployment of government personnel to monitor compliance and take action if necessary. Further, this component requires not only an adequate number of personnel but also sufficient competence and access to information. To assist in enactment, governments may engage in partnerships with schools, teachers' unions, the media and community bodies. They may also encourage tutoring providers to engage in self-regulation through industry professional associations and other ways; and they may seek to empower consumers so that these consumers can acquire pertinent information on tutoring providers and their behaviour.

2 What Needs to Be Regulated, Why and How?

2.1 An expanding phenomenon

Various publications have documented the scale of shadow education around the world (e.g. Bray & Lykins, 2012; Aurini et al., 2013; Park et al., 2016; Entrich, 2020; Bray, 2021a, 2021b; Bray & Hajar, 2023), and Appendix 1 presents some details from countries in all continents. In view of the expansion and changing nature of shadow education, an updated version of Bray's (2009, p. 24) grouping of countries is useful for understanding the global picture.

- *East Asia* is among the regions where tutoring is most prevalent and deeply rooted, and with a particularly long history in Japan and South Korea. Tutoring in Hong Kong and then Mainland China became evident at a later stage but scaled up rapidly. East Asian societies are highly competitive and hierarchical. Shadow education in such societies has been driven by high-stakes examinations and the differential impact of cultural traditions that value diligence, emphasise family obligations and uphold elitism, combined with neoliberal changes (Zhang & Yamato, 2018).

  Most countries have significant internal disparities among different geographic regions. In Mainland China, for example, data on private tutoring received by primary and secondary students (Grades 1-12) from the nationwide representative sample in the China Family Panel Studies (CFPS) indicated that 46.8% of students with urban residence and 16.9% of students with rural residence received tutoring (Liu & Bray, 2017).[1] Disparities in East Asia are also very evident across income groups (Kim & Park, 2010; Zhang & Bray, 2016; Entrich, 2018). Moreover, the quality of tutoring varies greatly depending on the forms and tutors. Effective tutoring is more accessible for affluent families and those with greater social capital.

- Private tutoring is also significant in many other *lower-income Asian countries* such as Bangladesh, Vietnam, India and Cambodia. In these settings, it has particularly been driven by low teachers' incomes, accompanied, especially in India, by the marketisation of the sector (see e.g. Bray et al., 2016; Punjabi, 2020; Joshi, 2021; Mahmud, 2021; Nguyen et al., 2021).
- In *former Soviet countries and Eastern Europe*, private tutoring already existed before the political transitions in the late 1980s and early 1990s, but pressures on teachers to supply tutoring – and then to engineer demand – expanded as a result of the collapse of economies and sharp decreases in the purchasing power of teachers' salaries (see e.g. Silova et al. 2006; Silova, 2010; Ahmadova, 2015; Šťastný, 2016; Khaydarov, 2020; Mikhaylova, 2022). Once private tutoring had become established, it remained a social norm.
- Researchers in the *Middle East* have documented significant rates of shadow education in the 1980s and 1990s in such countries as Bahrain, Iraq, Jordan and Kuwait (Bray & Hajar, 2023). More recently it has also emerged as a significant issue in Qatar and the United Arab Emirates. Some of these countries have even higher per capita incomes than Japan and South Korea, again showing that shadow education may be evident in prosperous as well as low-income countries.
- *African countries* have seen an increase in private tutoring, the supply of which is greatly driven by underpaid mainstream teachers (Bray, 2021b). Egypt has a long history of the phenomenon, with regulations dating from the 1940s (Egypt, 1947), i.e. even earlier than the counterpart regulations in South Korea (Lee et al., 2010). Mauritius also has a long history of policy concern (see e.g. Joynathsing et al., 1988; Foondun, 1992), but elsewhere in sub-Saharan Africa, the existence of large-scale private tutoring is more recent.
- In *North America, Australasia and Western Europe* private tutoring has also been long evident but limited in scope, in part because schooling has been perceived to be able to meet the main needs. However, increasing social competition has significantly changed the picture (Buchmann et al., 2010; Aurini et al., 2013; Davis, 2013; Dooley et al., 2020; Bray, 2021a). The participation rate in some Western European countries has grown substantially since the turn of the century with the increase in competition and social acceptance of the phenomenon.
- Demand for tutoring has also long been, and remains, high in parts of *Southern Europe*. In Greece, for example, a 2000 survey of 3,441 first-year university students found that 80% had attended

preparatory tutoring schools, half had received one-to-one tutoring, and 33% had taken both types of tutoring (Psacharopoulos & Papakonstantinou, 2005, p. 105). A decade later, nearly 60% of secondary students were attending tutoring institutes known as *frontistiria* (Kassotakis & Verdis, 2013, p. 99). In Cyprus, a 2003 survey indicated that 74% of households arranged tutoring for their children, and in 2009 proportions were 69% for primary school children and 82% for secondary school children (Lamprianou & Afantiti-Lamprianou, 2013, pp. 40–41).
- *Northern Europe* with arguably the world's strongest and most equitable public schooling, has long been protected from shadow education. However, recent changes brought by privatisation in the public system and increasing local and global competition as perceived by parents have facilitated the emergence of the phenomenon (see e.g. Christensen & Zhang, 2021; Kosunen et al., 2021).
- Finally, *Latin America* has had much lower rates of private tutoring, but it is emerging there too (see e.g. Galvão, 2020). In Argentina, Cámara and Gertel (2016) surveyed university freshmen admitted to four schools of a national university in 2013, and found that 36.4% had used private supplementary tutoring provided by individuals or private companies to prepare for end-of-secondary-schooling examinations.

From this global summary, significant variations are evident; but in many countries, well over half of student bodies enrol in some sort of tutoring, and in some societies, the figure exceeds 90%. As such, private supplementary tutoring has become a part of daily life for millions of families around the globe. Indeed for many families, private tutoring has become part of the educational process, not just an extra. It is driven by social competition, particularly during the build-up to high-stakes examinations but also working back from senior secondary to lower secondary and then to primary and even kindergarten education.

2.2 Regulating for social protection

The expanding reach of shadow education arguably increases the need for regulatory protection of individuals, families, communities and whole societies (Neto-Mendes, 2008). In this respect, the domain of tutoring may be compared with other service industries. The restaurant industry, for example, is regulated to ensure basic hygiene and prohibition of inappropriate additives; taxis and other forms of public transport are regulated for vehicle roadworthiness and driving skills;

and private clinics are regulated to ensure qualified medical practitioners and appropriate physical facilities. Consumers of private tutoring benefit from regulations when they can have confidence in the services, and whole societies benefit when regulations secure oversight of safety and social development.

In this connection, Bray and Kwo (2014) presented five reasons for regulating shadow education, focusing on what may be called the common good:

- *Social inequalities.* When left completely to market forces, shadow education is likely to maintain and exacerbate social inequalities. Particularly obvious are socioeconomic inequalities, since prosperous families can afford more and better-quality support than lower-income counterparts; but also pertinent are gender, racial/ethnic and rural/urban imbalances. Competitive families may engage in what in England has been called an "education arms race" (Weale, 2018), demanding other families to join the competition to avoid being left behind. In some settings, families feel forced to invest in shadow education even when the educational benefits are unclear (Box 2.1).

Box 2.1 What about the effectiveness of private tutoring?

An obvious question not only for families but also for governments and other stakeholders is whether shadow education "works" in the sense of improving students' examination scores and other outcomes. Much research has been devoted to this question (e.g. Loyalka & Zakharov, 2016; Kim & Hong, 2018; Guill et al., 2020), using a range of statistical techniques. However, the research encounters methodological challenges in separating the impact of shadow education from other variables (see Bray, 2014). In practice, much depends on the skills and motivations of the tutor, the readiness and motivations of the students, and the matches of tutoring curricula and modes of delivery with students' needs and aptitudes. A further set of variables arises when tutoring substitutes for schooling because students cease to pay so much attention in school or perhaps even become truants from school.

Nevertheless, regardless of whether shadow education does actually work, many families either assume that it works and/or decide to invest in it because everybody else seems to be doing so and they do not want to risk being left behind. And whether or not it works, the sector still needs to be regulated for the multitude of reasons presented here.

- *Backwash on regular schooling.* Shadow education is not just a shadow: it also affects the body that it imitates. The dynamics of classrooms are changed when some students receive tutoring but others do not. Shadow education may be beneficial for classroom environments if it reduces gaps, but in practice it commonly increases gaps; and teachers may assume that students receive tutoring, and therefore devote less effort to their classes than they would otherwise. Also, students may be tired in school from too much after-school tutoring; and they may be bored during school time if they have already learned the content in advance during tutoring.
- *Corruption.* Teachers who provide tutoring may devote more effort to their private lessons than to their regular classes for which they are paid regardless of quality; and teachers who tutor their existing students may deliberately "save" some materials from their regular lessons in order to promote the market for their services. If not permitted to tutor their own students, teachers may "trade" students with colleagues.
- *Protection of consumers and employees.* Even specialists encounter challenges in evaluating the quality of tutoring, and parents who work in other fields and perhaps themselves have limited education encounter even greater challenges. The consumers include the students themselves, who may be subjected to inappropriate overt and hidden advertising. Further, regulations may be needed for protection against sexual abuse in one-to-one locations. Turning to employees, the main category comprises the tutors themselves. Many companies employ tutors on a part-time basis, and university students working as tutors may have little experience of the sorts of conditions to which they should be entitled. Proper contracts are needed with both consumers and employees.
- *Taxation.* Since they are businesses like others, it seems reasonable to ask tutoring providers to pay taxes in the same way. This matter builds on the need for proper contracts, and also requires proper accounts.

In practice, some categories of shadow education are easier to regulate than others. Most regulations around the world focus on commercial companies that provide tutoring and on teachers in regular schools who desire to offer private tutoring alongside their core work. In countries where after-school programmes are outsourced to tutoring providers, regulations may also focus on non-profit organisations of various kinds. Tutoring provided informally, e.g. by university students in the homes of the tutees on a one-to-one basis, is much more difficult to regulate and is generally set aside. Since the authorities are unable to impose regulations on these informal operations, an alternative approach is to empower consumers to set performance indicators and demand accountability.

2.3 Regulating companies that provide tutoring

A number of categories for possible regulation may be listed as follows:

1. *Registration*. A first requirement is that companies should register their existence. This may be with the Ministry of Education and/or the Ministry of Commerce or equivalent. In Denmark, for example, tutoring companies are registered as corporations with the Danish Business Authority, and additional registrations are required as child-related businesses. The Ukrainian and Russian authorities have a different model with an educational licence being required for tutoring institutions (Ukraine Parliament, 2000; Russian Federation, 2013). In Mainland China, tutoring enterprises may only provide services after having obtained both educational and business licenses at the county/district level (Zhang, 2019). Local governments are in charge of inspection and monitoring before and after the issue of Certificates of Registration as Tutoring Institutions.

    An initial question concerns the threshold at which operators are required to register and obtain licences. In Macao (China), the threshold is defined as an establishment providing lessons to seven or more people at any one time, or 21 or more people on any one day (Macao, 2002, Article 5). In neighbouring Hong Kong (China), the regulation is similar but has a threshold of eight people at any one time or 20 people in one day (Hong Kong, 2003, p. 1). In South Korea, tutoring institutions serving 10 or more students simultaneously must be registered as *hagwons* (tutoring enterprises) (Piao & Hwang, 2021). Another type that requires registration in South Korea is *gyoseup so* (tutoring centres), which embraces tutoring classes for nine or fewer students simultaneously in only one subject. Registration of self-employed tutors is not required, but they need to submit an attestation of no-child-abuse records to the education authorities and are prohibited from tutoring more than nine students simultaneously. In Japan, home tutors and *juku* providing services for more than two months are subject to the law on specified commercial transactions as providers of specified continuous services (Japan, Government, 1976; Zhang, 2018).

Registration brings tutoring providers out of the shadows and is the starting point for regulation. Policies on registration in South Korea and Japan show awareness and respect for the diversity of tutoring providers. By specifying requirements for different categories of tutoring providers, the regulations bring self-employed tutors and small tutoring centres out of the shadows since ignoring their existence would push them to the black market. Of course, in enactment, some providers may manage to evade registration, particularly if they are self-employed and thereby avoid taxation and other responsibilities. However, such informality and evasion undermine their legitimacy. Thus while registration is a basic starting point for the authorities, it can also bring benefits to the entrepreneurs.

2. *Premises.* Regulation of premises is another sensible starting point for authorities that plan to bring more control and order into the tutoring sector. Physical premises are relatively easy to define and to measure, though of course questions remain about precisely what should be regulated. Companies that provide tutoring on their own premises are normally required to meet regulations for basic health and safety – fire escapes, hygiene, noise, etc. These would be requirements for companies of all types, not just education companies. In addition, some authorities have educational requirements, e.g. for space/area per student. For example:

- In *Ethiopia*, the Addis Ababa Education Bureau requires tutoring premises to have minimum areas of 600 square metres (Bray, 2021b, p. 32).
- The *Uzbekistan* government permits institutions to be located in detached premises, built-in rooms or attached rooms but states that the buildings should not exceed three storeys in most cities or four storeys in large cities. In addition, staircase handrails should be at least 1.2 metres high (Uzbekistan, 2013).
- In *China*, local Fire Departments have regulations on fire escapes for tutoring companies, and the national guideline for classroom accommodation is "above three square metres per tutee for all tutees receiving tutoring at the same premises at the same time" (China, General Office of the State

Council, 2018). Tutorial companies are forbidden to operate in residential properties, and most local authorities require providers to operate in commercial properties and to have no less than 300 square metres (or 200 metres in some jurisdictions). This requirement has become a threshold for tutoring providers, leading to closure of small centres and driving others underground (Zhang, 2019).

- The *Russian* government requires classrooms to have at least 2 square metres per tutee; and levels of noise, vibration, ultrasound, infrasound, electromagnetic fields and radiation in tutoring institutions should not exceed standards for public buildings and residential areas (Russian Federation, Ministry of Health, 2014).

3. *Personnel.* One major question is whether tutors should have professional qualifications. The Malaysian government stipulates that tutors must have a teaching permit and that principals/managers must have at least three years of working experience or at least six months in a related field (Kenayathulla, 2013). In South Korea, all professional tutors and *hagwon* managers that conduct teaching must be registered with documentary evidence of educational qualifications and no criminal record. The government has set standards for minimum tutor qualifications. Tutors in *hagwons* and *gyoseup so* must hold community college degrees or above, but there is no qualification requirement for self-employed private tutors. Teachers are prohibited from tutoring. The Chinese government also requires tutors to hold teaching certificates, specifically for the subjects in which they tutor (China, Ministry of Education [MoE], 2018); and the Ukraine government requires tutors to be certified every five years (Ukraine, Parliament, 2000). In Iraq, the number of personnel establishing a tutorial centre should not be less than three, among whom at least one must hold a bachelor's degree in education and the others must hold at least a middle/intermediate school certificate (Iraq, Ministry of Education, 2017a).

The Russian government took a step further with detailed standards for teachers and tutors in five categories: Tutor of supplementary education, Senior tutor of supplementary education, Trainer-teacher, Senior trainer-teacher and Teacher (Russian Federation, Ministry of Labour and Social Protection, 2018). The ladders provide recognition for tutor identity and professional development. In some societies where teachers and

What Needs to Be Regulated, Why and How? 23

schools are prohibited from providing tutoring, such as China, Japan and South Korea, tutoring companies are in turn prohibited from hiring school teachers (Zhang & Yamato, 2018; Zhang, 2019). Governments elsewhere are more relaxed on these matters.

Another question relates to child abuse. In Denmark, attestations of no-criminal-record (*Straffeattest*) and no-child-abuse-record (*Childrenattest*) are mandatory for teachers/tutors and other personnel working with children. Similarly, legislation in Western Australia prohibits work with children by people who have been charged with or convicted of certain child-related offences (Western Australia, Department of Education, 2004). In response to the suicide of a famous writer due to rape by her tutor, the government in Taiwan (China) amended its regulations attaching great importance to the sexual criminal attestations. The Taiwan government also established a database of people with criminal records who should be forbidden from tutoring.

4. *Contracts.* Companies are commonly required to have proper written contracts not only with their employees but also with their clients. Regulations on contracts with clients provide legal basis for consumer protection and disputes. China's Ministry of Education, working jointly with the State Administration for Market Regulation, has released a sample contract for tutoring companies to consider. The purposes are to guide tutoring companies in preparing contracts, and to protect consumers. It mirrors almost all domains of regulations, reflecting the well-intended yet over-ambitious state intervention. *Jukus* in Japan should follow regulations on termination of contract by clients. In the case of termination of contract during a programme, *jukus* can charge half the fees for the month of termination if the tutee attended classes for up to half of the month. Further regulations (Japan, Government, 2000) allow *jukus* to charge penalties equivalent to tutoring fees for the following month or 20,000 yen, whichever is the lower (Zhang, 2018).

5. *Advertising.* Regulations may aim to prevent false claims on websites, posters, flyers, etc. In Hong Kong (China), for example, the Consumer Council has prepared advice on the types of advertising that are unacceptable, with examples of exaggerated and trick wording (Bray & Kwo, 2014, pp. 42–43); and tutoring providers in Japan are subject to the Act against Unjustifiable Premiums and Misleading Representations (Japan, Government, 1962) and the Unfair Competition Prevention Act (Japan, Government, 1993) (Box 2.2).

> **Box 2.2 Violations of Japan's Act against Unjustifiable Premiums and Misleading Representations**
>
> In 2014, Japan's Consumer Affairs Agency took action against a *juku* deemed to have violated the Act against Unjustifiable Premiums and Misleading Representations. The *juku* had operated nationwide, with advertisements to recruit students for summer and winter programmes. Photos of the company's tutors with their names and those of the institutions from which they had allegedly graduated had been posted with such descriptions as:
>
> - 98% of tutors are elite graduates from national and public universities or colleges, and
> - elite tutors who have received rigorous training.
>
> In fact, only 14% of the company's tutors had graduated from national and public universities or colleges, and 83.5% of the tutors were undergraduates in national and public universities working part-time in the *juku*. Statements about "graduates from" were false advertising, not only because they had not graduated but also because consumers could be misled into viewing them as full-time rather than part-time tutors.

In their advertising, tutorial institutions should be mindful of rights concerning portraits, privacy, trademarks, designs, trade names, copyright and publicity (Zhang, 2018). In response to the vicious advertising competition between big companies, the Chinese national government set a ceiling on advertising expenses at 3% of the sales revenue of academic tutoring institutions (China, National Development and Reform Commission [NDRC], 2021).

6. *Hours of Operation.* A problem arises when tutoring activities compete with schooling, most obviously by operating at the same time but also by operating late in the evening and thereby causing students to be tired the next day in school.

- The *Korean* authorities have set curfews on the hours at which tutorial companies may operate (Choi & Cho, 2016). Table 2.1 shows variations in the curfew requirement by levels of education and locations. The later curfew for upper secondary students reflects consideration about pressures from college admission. The enforcement of curfews is labour-intensive. Government personnel were sent to check late at night and to

Table 2.1 Curfews on Tutoring Companies in South Korea, by Location and Level of Education

	Level of Education		
Primary	Lower Secondary	Upper Secondary	Province/Municipality
		22.00	Seoul, Daegu, Gwangju, Gyeonggi
21.00	22.00	22.00	Sejong
21.00	22.00	23.00	Incheon, Jeonbuk
21.00	23.00	24.00	Chungnam, Gyeongbuk, Gyeongnam, Jeju
22.00	23.00	24.00	Daejeon, Gangwon
22.00	22.00	23.00	Busan
22.00	22.00	23.50	Jeollanam-do
23.00	23.00	24.00	Chungbuk
		24.00	Ulsan

Source: Piao (2020).

ask students to go home, yet some tutoring continued underground beyond the curfew. Also, some tutoring providers partially evaded the curfews by moving their tutees from regions with earlier curfews to those with later ones.

- In *Mainland China*, when the curfew for tutorial classes was set at 8.30 pm some companies proceeded with online tutoring after 8.30 pm. Thus, further regulations were released to set a curfew on online tutoring at 9.00 pm. Unlike South Korea, where the tutoring time specified by the regulations was from 5.00 am till the time of the curfew (i.e. including school hours), the Chinese regulations stated that tutoring schedules should not conflict with official school hours. This measure was a response to cases of students skipping schooling to receive tutoring.
- Counterpart regulations in *Russia* (Russian Federation, 2014) and *Uzbekistan* (Uzbekistan, 2013) went further to recommend time limits with consideration of seasonal variations and durations of classes and breaks. For instance, the Russian document stated that tutoring classes should start no earlier than 8.00 am and conclude no later than 8.00 pm, except for students aged 16–18 who could finish classes at 9.00 pm. Further, the document recommended (but did not require) that tutoring classes on school days last no more than three hours per day, and during weekends and vacations last no more than four hours per day. A break for at least 10 minutes was recommended after 30–45 minutes of class time.

- With a different orientation, authorities in *Sri Lanka* have prohibited tutorial companies from operating on Buddhist festival days and on Sundays between 8.00 am and 2.00 pm (Bray & Kwo, 2014, p. 44).

7. *Class size.* Regulations issued in Ethiopia by the Addis Ababa Education Bureau (albeit largely ignored) stated that tutorial classes should have no more than 10 students (Bray, 2021b, p. 58). In Hong Kong (China), by contrast, the maximum is 45 students (Hong Kong, 2012). The Uzbekistan government states that tutoring classes can be held individually or in groups, with the latter being single-age or mixed-age. Group occupancy in tutoring institutions for children is "not recommended" to exceed 15 children (Uzbekistan, 2013). In some countries, class size is constrained indirectly by requirements on area per student as explained above.
8. *Affordability and financial management.* Concerned about social inequalities, some authorities have set ceilings on fees. The Korean government is an example. It requires all tutoring providers to publicise information on tutoring fees and to issue receipts. In 2008, the government established a Call Centre hotline through which parents could complain if they had been overcharged. In China, tutoring companies are prohibited from charging fees for periods exceeding three months. In both countries (academic) tutoring is subject to price control, i.e. the guidance price set by provincial governments based on the variations in class size, duration of tutoring, etc. (China, NDRC, 2021; Piao & Hwang, 2021).
9. *Curriculum and tutoring materials.* Some governments wish to control the curriculum of tutorial companies, to ensure that it does not greatly diverge from the curriculum in schools (see e.g. Pakistan, 2013, clause 4(a)). They may want the tutoring curriculum to follow school curriculum goals and standards for quality assurance and to be less examination-oriented. They may also be concerned about the pace of tutoring, considering it undesirable for students to learn content ahead of schooling because it may create inequalities in school classrooms and lead the students to feel bored when hearing the materials again. Considering the study load on students and vicious competition accelerated by tutoring ahead of school curricula, the Chinese government prohibits tutoring companies from providing training for Olympiads and similar competitions, and requires the tutoring curriculum to follow the same pace as the school curriculum. In contrast to

What Needs to Be Regulated, Why and How? 27

this "hard" regulation, the Russian government has taken a softer approach by indicating what is desirable as the content and purpose of tutoring. Item 4 of Order of the Ministry of Education of the Russian Federation (2018) specified that tutoring should aim for the development of creativity; meeting the individual needs and interests of students that are outside federal state educational standards and federal government requirements; creating a learning culture and culture of healthy and safe lifestyles; socialisation; providing spiritual and moral, civil-patriotic, military-patriotic, labour education of students and identify, develop and support talented learners as well as those who have shown outstanding ability. As noted by Ostromukhova (2016), supplemental education (with some exceptions) is understood as a "continuous process of self-development and self-improvement of the person as a subject of culture and activity".

10. *Organisational structure.* In Uzbekistan (Uzbekistan, 1995) and Kazakhstan (Kazakhstan, 2013) tutoring institutions are required to create "pedagogical councils", i.e. collegiate bodies that bring together the tutors for professional development and for discussion on curriculum and instructional approaches. The Uzbekistan document adds that the highest governing bodies for tutoring institutions are the collective meetings. Delegates with the right to vote are elected by assemblies of educators, older students and parents. The Kazakhstan regulations prohibit the operation of political and religious activities in tutoring institutions.

11. *Application of technology in registration, certification, monitoring and consumer protection.* In countries where the scale of tutoring is large and regulations are relatively fierce, technologies are applied for enforcement of laws and regulations. In South Korea, the government has set up online platforms for digital registration of *hagwons* and tutors (Korea, 2020b), and for online reports of illegal practices that violate the laws and regulations with monetary rewards (Korea, 2020a). China has also launched national and local online platforms for managing tutoring institutions, which are used for digital registration of tutoring institutions, filing and inspection of tutoring curriculum and materials, report of illegal practices and information disclosure (China, 2019a). Some local authorities have used AI and big data technologies for site-check and monitoring of payment (see above Chinese regulation on fees).

In all these categories, however, a gap may be evident between the wording of the regulations and the enactment in practice.

Further, the majority of governments are *laissez faire* on these matters. Some authorities recognise constraints on their own capacity to monitor and regulate the sector, some consider shadow education as a solution to economic and educational problems, and others simply view the shadow education sector as beyond their remit because they consider themselves to be bodies principally responsible for schooling. The enactment of regulations is shaped by governments' commitment to enforce as well as tutoring providers' willingness to comply. For instance, governments with stronger commitment such as that of South Korea devote sustained and regular effort to reinforcing regulations. This approach creates social and political pressures for tutoring providers to respond and comply. Compared to self-employed tutors and small tutoring centres, medium-sized and big companies are more visible (and thus easier to identify and track). Therefore, these companies usually have more incentives and pressures to comply with regulations.

Regulating tutoring requires dealing not only with tutoring providers but also with tutoring consumers. In enactment, the failures mostly happen when some families support tutoring practices that violate regulations. Some parents and students who like the personality and/or style of tutors with whom they are acquainted may proceed with employment even if those tutors are untrained. Also, some parents want their children to study hard, even late in the evening, and are willing to hide from the authorities any infringement of regulations. Further, in countries as different as Japan and Egypt, parents have declared that just as schooling is a human right so is tutoring. The Japanese and Korean governments have long been concerned about the study burden on students; but since those governments have also respected parental rights to seek tutoring, the efforts to reduce the burden have been offset by parents wanting to sharpen their competitive edges.

2.4 Regulations on supplementary tutoring by teachers and schools

Questions whether serving teachers should be permitted to provide supplementary tutoring are controversial. Debate is especially vigorous when the teachers are in public schools, and situations are considered especially problematic when teachers provide tutoring to students for whom they are already responsible. As mentioned, commentators fear that teachers who provide supplementary tutoring will neglect their mainstream work, for which they are paid anyway, in order to devote attention to their private instruction. Further, teachers who are permitted to tutor their existing students may be tempted deliberately to cut content during regular lessons and leak information on school-based examinations to favour students who attend their extra classes. Such matters are linked to ethics and corruption (Bray, 2003; Dawson, 2009), and are among the factors underlying what Jayachandran (2014) has called "incentives to teach badly".

An initial question relates to the reasons that teachers provide tutoring. Box 2.3 presents the main reasons, among which financial ones dominate. It is arguable that regulations to prevent teachers from providing tutoring are unlikely to prevail so long as teachers have a genuine financial need to supplement their salaries. Under such circumstances, parents and other members of society are also likely to be sympathetic.

Box 2.3 What attracts teachers to tutoring?

Teachers' involvement in tutoring may have different forms, including direct provision, running tutorial centres and taking kickbacks for referrals. Financial motives are the major factor for teachers' involvement, but social and educational factors may also play important roles. Most teachers are involved in tutoring for mixed reasons.

Most obviously, teachers become involved in tutoring to supplement their incomes – either because their salaries are too low for basic family needs or because the teachers desire middle-class lifestyles in settings dominated by consumerism. In Cambodia, for instance, many teachers consider income from tutoring to be necessary for basic living, and the teachers who do not provide tutoring have other income sources e.g. from grocery shops or farming. In countries such as the UK and USA where teachers are arguably well paid, some teachers still become involved in tutoring. For most of these teachers, the extra income is not for making ends meet but for "quality life" including cars, housing and medical care.

Teachers also provide tutoring for professional freedom. They use teaching methods and materials that may not be accepted in schools and select their own students. Some teachers value the recognition and a sense of achievement in tutoring that they cannot get in schools.

Time is another factor in some settings, related to school workloads. In Hong Kong (China), many teachers who do not provide tutoring reported that they were already overloaded by teaching and administration. During the COVID-19 crisis when schools were suspended,

> teachers in many countries turned to tutoring because they had free time. COVID-19 increased teacher involvement in the UK and USA: teachers who had not previously provided tutoring started to do so and were welcomed or even driven by parents who were upset by disrupted schooling.
>
> A related factor concerns curriculum and evaluation. In Cambodia, double-shift schooling constrains class time. Many teachers find it difficult to finish even the core curriculum within school hours, let alone additional exercises. Thus, some teachers and schools treat tutoring as an extension of schooling in order to maintain students' performance. In Mainland China, some high-performing teachers have tutored only their own students in order to maintain their reputations in systems that evaluate teachers according to their students' examination grades and promotion rates.
>
> Social values also matter in teachers' decisions. In cultures where a teacher's involvement in tutoring is widely accepted or taken for granted, teachers do not have to worry about social consequences. In Greece, for example, prestigious teachers get double benefits in the tutoring market: both income and reinforcement of their reputations. By contrast, Japanese teachers in public schools worry about the damage that tutoring would cause to the reputations of both teachers and schools.
>
> Finally, some teachers provide tutoring because of power relations. Case studies in China have shown that a few teachers have provided tutoring because they have not dared to reject their school managers or parents. Related, other studies show that teachers provide tutoring in exchange for favours.

Bray and Kwo (2014, pp. 44–45) documented four government approaches to regulating teachers' involvement in private supplementary tutoring: prohibition, discouragement, permission if approved and *laissez faire*. In settings where teachers provide tutoring, schools are also usually involved to some extent. Thus either officially or unofficially, schools are involved in the provision of private supplementary tutoring in countries as diverse as Australia, Cambodia, Czech Republic, Kenya, Turkey, the United Arab Emirates and Uzbekistan.

Prohibitions of serving teachers from providing tutoring may be found across world regions (see e.g. Bray & Kwo, 2014; Bray, 2021c). In Sub-Saharan Africa, for example, prohibitions have been issued in such countries as Eritrea, The Gambia, Kenya, Zambia and Zimbabwe. In the Middle East and North Africa, they may be found in Egypt, Kuwait, Oman and Palestine; and in Asia, prohibitions have been issued in Bhutan, China, Japan, Myanmar and South Korea. In Taiwan (China), rapid growth of tutoring after 1968 was largely absorbed by small enterprises known locally as *buxiban* and mainly staffed by school teachers working on a supplementary basis. The educational authority issued regulations prohibiting in-service teachers from tutoring and *buxiban* from hiring teachers. To reinforce the regulations, government personnel conducted periodic and ad hoc monitoring visits to *buxiban* and schools. Teachers who were found to have infringed the regulation lost their jobs. Following the enforcement of these regulations, small *buxiban* staffed by school teachers almost disappeared after the 1990s and were replaced by *buxiban* run by tutoring professionals. The government established a reporting mechanism to receive complaints if teachers were found to be providing tutoring.

Similar strong prohibitions on teachers providing private supplementary tutoring were enforced in Japan. Following the introduction of these regulations, some teachers left schooling for shadow education; but in any case, as shadow education became more professional and independent from schooling, the demand for school teachers sharply declined. Many *juku* felt that school teachers were not actually qualified for tutoring because it required different skills from those in public schools. Like their counterparts in Taiwan (China), the authorities created a reporting mechanism for complaints, and the Ministry of Education publicises cases of teacher malpractice on its website.

Some governments, such as those of Myanmar and Iraq, go beyond general pronouncements by asking teachers to sign documents indicating that they are aware of the prohibition and will not infringe it (Bray et al., 2020, p. 24; Iraq, 2017b). However, teachers in Myanmar commonly take the procedure as a formality that can be ignored in practice. Salaries are low, and even officials in the hierarchy may be willing to "turn a blind eye" to the continued provision of private tutoring by serving teachers. In any case, the penalties in Myanmar for infringing the regulations are harsh to the point of being unrealistic: a fine of 300,000 kyats (US$200) or three years in jail or both. Both teachers and government officers know that a huge outcry would occur if a teacher were jailed for two years simply for giving extra lessons (which many people view as a good thing to do).

Also pertinent is that in reality, even governments may see practical benefits from teachers providing tutoring. As in Myanmar, the Cambodian authorities are overtly critical of teachers' provision of tutoring but in practice may tacitly accept, not least because the ability to earn extra incomes keeps at least some teachers in the profession despite the low government salaries, and assists the government to achieve its Education for All goals (Bray et al., 2016).

An alternative approach is to allow teachers to provide tutoring under certain conditions. The following categories fit under this heading:

1. *Registration.* Teachers who offer private supplementary tutoring may in some jurisdictions be required to register. This is the case in Malaysia, where additional stipulations include (Malaysia, Government, 2006, Section 4) that:

    - the applicant is a government employee confirmed in the post;
    - an application for approval has been made at least two months in advance;
    - the applicant has annual performance scores of 80% or more in the previous year;
    - the tutoring is not conducted in a Centre owned by a family member; and
    - tutoring does not interfere with duties as a teacher and is conducted outside working hours.

    The authorities in Brunei Darussalam similarly require advance approval (Mahdini, 2009).

2. *Premises.* Some governments prohibit private tutoring on the premises of public schools on the grounds that they are public property and should not be exploited for personal gain. This is the policy in Tanzania and Zimbabwe, for example (Anangisye, 2016, p. 8; Bray, 2021b, p. 61). However, other governments permit and even encourage private tutoring on school premises on the grounds that the facilities have been constructed for educational use and that children are safer in such locations than in converted garages and other potentially unsuitable premises (see Bray, 2009, p. 57 for the example of Mauritius). In Tunisia, 2015 regulations restricted private tutoring to the school premises, with permission from the principals and district education offices (Tunisia, 2015).

3. *Durations and Days of Tutoring.* The Singapore government allows teachers to provide tutoring, and about 10% do so. However, the provision is limited to six hours per week (Lu, 2004; Singapore, Ministry of Education, 2019). A similar provision exists in Malaysia with a limit of four hours per week (Malaysia, 2006, Section 4).

The government of Chongqing municipality in China used to prohibit teachers from tutoring on schools' working days, though later the policy was replaced by complete prohibition in line with national government policy. Teachers were required to sign statements showing awareness of the policies. Schools secured the signed statements and submitted to the local education commission for the record.

4. *Personnel.* Some governments that permit teachers to offer tutoring nevertheless prohibit them from tutoring the students for whom they are already responsible. Regulations in the Maldives also prohibit teachers from tutoring other students in the same grade of their schools (Maldives, Ministry of Education 2002 *Guidelines for Teachers*, cited in Mariya, 2012, p. 164).

Again, however, the majority of governments are *laissez faire* on these matters. They leave matters to market forces and to the discretion of families, teachers and schools, chiefly because they do not wish to get entangled with political forces and perhaps with regulations that they cannot enforce. The attitude of one government officer in Rwanda seems to have wide relevance. This officer stated that he preferred to leave matters to the school level, and added (Bray, 2021b, p. 62):

> We are also parents; we understand the need for extra studies for children. We understand that each child has a special way of studying.

For these and related reasons, even when regulations do exist they may not be followed closely.

2.5 Tutoring providers in public-private partnerships

Public-Private Partnerships (PPPs) have become increasingly evident in this domain (Bray & Zhang, 2018). Much can be learned from other sectors not only about trust and management (see e.g. Warsen et al., 2018) but also about inadequacy of oversight and unbalanced agendas (see e.g. Sherratt et al., 2020). Concerning shadow education, PPPs have a range of contexts and objectives, and therefore diversity in regulations. PPPs in shadow education have three major modes: (1) after-school programmes and subsidies initiated by governments at the system level, (2) school purchase of tutoring services at the institutional level and (3) Corporate Social Responsibility (CSR) and charity by tutoring institutions. The second and third modes will be elaborated in the Japan and China chapters. Concerning the first mode, the following are particularly worth noting:

- *Australia.* The government of Western Australia (2018) has stressed that principals and teachers are responsible for students' educational programmes, but also recognises that schools do not always have the necessary resources to meet the full range of needs. In such circumstances, the government recognises (p. 3), "the principal may consider requests from parents to grant approval for students to attend private tutoring during school hours". These activities may be on or off the school premises. Private tutoring programmes during school hours must (p. 4):
  - be confined to activities that enrich the content of the school's educational programme;
  - address the particular educational needs of students in areas not provided by the school; and
  - not replace regular school educational programmes.

  Principals must be satisfied that each private tutor is appropriately qualified and has had a National Criminal Record History Check (NCRHC) and a Working with Children Check (WWCC). Tutors must have public liability insurance of AUD5 million, and have written agreements with the students' parents or guardians. The overall emphasis is on tutors filling gaps on what schools cannot provide, and on clarity about professional obligations and legal protection.

  Also worth noting is the scheme prepared for the State of Victoria in 2020 to help children compensate for learning lost during the COVID-19 pandemic. This scheme, with a budget of AUD230 million, was designed to provide 4,100 places for pre-service, retired and occasional teachers to work with schools. In the words of the Chief Executive Officer (CEO) of the Australian Tutoring Association (Dhall, 2020), it was a way to avoid a situation in which "you have two systems that distrust one another rather than engage". He viewed this tutoring as "the way to remediate learning loss and to give equity and access to low-income families", while also stressing the need for tutors to be qualified and accountable. A similar scheme with a budget of AUD337 to employ 5,500 personnel was subsequently launched in New South Wales (Smith, 2020), with the possibility of becoming a long-term arrangement (Baker, 2020).

- *South Korea.* In contrast to Western Australia, Korean policies have been devised in the context of longstanding and far-reaching out-of-school tutoring through *hagwons* and other arrangements. After-School Programmes (ASPs) operated on school premises seek to provide low-cost support to students and families, and to obviate the need for students to utilise private-sector offerings. As explained by Lee (2011, p. 17), a 2004 reform revised existing arrangements to allow schools to design the curricula, hire instructors from either within or outside the schools and charge small fees. Initially, schools were not permitted to make contracts with for-profit providers, but this restriction was later removed.

    Evaluations of ASPs are not entirely consistent but generally point in the same direction. Park et al. (2012, p. 3) suggested that students in Grades 8 to 10 who had attended ASPs did not significantly raise their academic performance but did have better relationships with teachers and friends, and spent less money on private tutoring in higher grades. Using a different data set, Carr and Wang (2017, p. 887) calculated that each additional hour of ASP displaced almost a complete hour of unassisted study (22 minutes) plus private tutoring (32 minutes), adding that families were not willing completely to disengage with private tutoring in the context of social norms and a perception that the ASPs were not total substitutes in content. They added that each additional ASP hour reduced the share of household income devoted to private tutoring by 0.5%; and since the mean number of ASP hours was 4.6, this equated to an average monthly reduction of 2.3%.

    Alongside these programmes, free tutoring has been delivered through the Educational Broadcasting System (EBS), sometimes employing famous tutors from the private sector. The EBS traces its history to the launch in 1974 of the Radio School, and by stages developed in reach and prestige (Korea Educational Broadcasting System [EBS], 2020). The value of the EBS was further demonstrated in 2020 when the COVID-19 pandemic closed schools and thus their face-to-face instruction.
- *Japan.* The Japanese government has sought to use PPPs to reduce income gaps and to enhance academic performance. Publicly-funded after school programmes are provided in public facilities in partnerships between non-profit organisations, *jukus* and local community members such as retired teachers, college students and elderly with knowledge in arts, music, local histories, etc. (Kuroishi & Takahashi, 2009; Japan, Ministry of Education, Culture, Sports, Science and Technology [MEXT], 2015). Some

regional governments have also contracted *jukus* to provide lifelong learning classes for local communities (Zhang & Yamato, 2018, p. 328).

Elaborating, historical analysis shows initiatives by different government bodies and diverse providers. The Ministry of Health, Labour & Welfare (MHLW) and MEXT have both funded after-school programmes. The MHLW launched the "after-school classrooms for children" scheme in the early 2000s. The initial goal was to provide public venues and care for children of working parents after school. The scheme evolved into a programme to promote learning activities at school and other public venues during after-school time, weekends and holidays under the wider MEXT initiative, *Chiiki Mirai Juku* (local learning programmes for the future). Subsequently, the initiative was further broadened into MEXT's "school-home-community" plan to strengthen partnerships between schools, families and local communities.

The initiative provided free support for children in low-income families. In addition to improving the academic achievements of low achievers, it aimed to revitalise local communities and promote lifelong learning. The costs were shared by national, provincial and local governments, each providing one-third of the funding.[2] Non-profit organisations (NPOs), *jukus* and community centres received funding for their services, while individual volunteers were not "paid" but usually received "honoraria" to cover expenses. No standard requirements were set for the content and modes of *mirai juku*, and local communities had autonomy to fit their local contexts. Some programmes were very diverse, ranging from supplementary tutoring, childcare and camping to sports and cultural events.

These programmes had shared goals of education equity. They were also government attempts to give students safe places, away from social problems such as violence and gambling. The programmes recruited tutors from the local communities, including *juku* tutors, private tutors, retired teachers and college students. They utilised public facilities including schools (outside official hours), libraries and community-based educational facilities (such as traditional community centres for social education) that would otherwise have been empty. In 2020, 17,066 schools (accounting for 60% of all schools in Japan) had established centres for *mirai juku* (Japan MEXT, 2020).

Mirai juku started with careful planning and good intentions, but encountered challenges and disparities in implementation.

At the local level, coordinators were drawn from the civil service, schools, community centres, or parents. MEXT and regional education authorities were mainly in charge of proposal reviews and grant approvals. MEXT officials also worked with local officials and coordinators to collect data and information, and establish platforms for local coordinators to share lessons and experiences. However, little monitoring and evaluation was conducted, and the effectiveness varied greatly according to resources and management capacities.

Case studies of *mirai juku* programmes by the author showed huge disparities. In some cities and districts, schools and community members were very supportive, while coordinators elsewhere encountered challenges to retain volunteers and organise activities. Although the *mirai juku* targeted children at risk, student participation was voluntary. As a result, students who used such services were mostly those from middle classes and without learning difficulties. Many children from low-income families and/or with learning difficulties were still left out.

- *Sweden*. In 2007, the government launched a household tax-deduction scheme which, among other features, permitted families to claim tax deductions for private tutoring (Lapidus, 2019; Hallsén, 2021; Karlsson, 2021). The scheme was abolished in 2015, but subsequent arrangements allowed schools and not-for-profit tutoring organisers to apply for funds. Empirical studies of these programmes show concerns about quality, partly due to curriculum weaknesses, challenges in cost-effectiveness and competition from shadow education. The original scheme was controversial because it seemed to favour families with a stronger initiative to access the funds rather than families that actually needed the funds, and because it channelled public resources to private enterprises. The revised scheme addressed some of these criticisms but remained controversial in the blurring of boundaries between public and private.

The 2007 scheme unintentionally drove the expansion of shadow education, evidenced in the rise and fall of a major Swedish tutoring company. The company was founded in 2005 and specialised in one-to-one home tutoring. It benefited from the rapidly-growing demand following the launch of the 2007 scheme, and became the largest tutoring company in Northern Europe. However, following the 2015 abolition of the government scheme its prices ceased to be attractive to many families. Due to the declining market and managerial difficulties, the company had to merge with another company for survival. Some small tutoring centres closed for similar reasons. However, private tutoring still had a market among parents who had become accustomed to it. Some parents chose tutoring companies over the free NPO services which they assessed as poorer in quality. By contrast, in Denmark a rising tutoring company expanded its business when the school-based tutoring programmes for lower achievers failed, since parents considered it as a stigma for their children and poorly managed.

- *England.* Like the society as a whole, English schools have increasingly recognised the potential roles of shadow education. In some cases, they have used government-provided money to employ tutors. One example reported by the press was a school in a low-income part of London (Coughlan, 2019). In the context of the COVID-19 crisis that led to the closure of schools in 2020, the authorities in England launched a year-long National Tutoring Programme (NTP) to help pupils catch up on lost learning (Education Endowment Foundation, 2020; Weale & Adams, 2020). Some schools used government funds to hire private tutors from approved agencies.

In its first year, the NTP was led by five charities and supported by several companies including the large accounting firm KPMG. Among these charities, the Education Endowment Foundation (EEF) provided "evidence" on the "substantial attainment gaps between pupils from disadvantaged backgrounds and their classmates" and suggested that the gaps were likely to grow significantly when schools were closed to most pupils. It provided "extensive evidence" on the impact of tutoring "to support pupils who have fallen behind" (Education Endowment Foundation, 2020); but much of this evidence could in fact be questioned.

In addition to the national story of how tutoring was necessary to support children during and beyond COVID-19, the NTP partners cited "experience" from other countries to steer the discourse in favour of publicly-funded tutoring programmes. A post on the official NTP page showcased "how other countries are responding to school closures" (Yeomans, 2021). The post only cited similar initiatives in the Netherlands (a two-year tutoring program funded by the Dutch government) and a paper (not research on national programmes) by authors in the USA, based on which national tutoring programmes were described as "global efforts". The post asserted that this US research presented a vision for tutoring "to become a core feature of the US education system, rather than just being a short-term response to Covid" (Yeomans, 2021).

However, no information was given on tutoring providers and the impact of such programmes on teachers and schools.

Certainly what the NTP partners aimed to achieve, as evidenced in other presentations, was to make the NTP a long-term institution in the English education system rather than a short-term solution. These actors were to be applauded for their efforts to improve education equity and learning support during COVID-19. However, simplistic optimism about tutoring as part of the school system risked legitimising and perpetuating private provision of tutoring in the long run and erosion of the roles of schools. Further, some entrepreneurs outsourced the tutoring to providers that were considered controversial. For example the press reported on one company that outsourced to tutors in Sri Lanka "who are as young as 17 and earning as little as £1.57 an hour" (Weale, 2021). The government responded by setting a minimum age of 18, but the nature of such marketisation remained controversial among some communities.

Ironically, advocacy in the USA for nationwide and "high-dosage" tutoring programmes in turn cited England's NTP to make the case (Barnum, 2020a; 2020b; Goldstein & Paulle, 2020). Government-funded tutoring programmes could reduce financial and learning gaps if carried out sensibly. However, careful planning is needed before the launch of such programmes not just in financing, effectiveness, monitoring and evaluation, but also in the nature and quality of tutoring providers. After all, PPPs between schools and private providers of tutoring aimed to supporting schools and families until the crisis subsided. In some settings they seemed more likely to trap schools and families in long-term reliance on tutoring that would have to be paid for either from their own pockets or by the governments through taxation.

- *USA.* A new era in educational history was brought by the 2001 No Child Left Behind (NCLB) Act, which operated until in 2015, it was replaced by the Every Child Succeeds Act (ESSA) (Lee, 2020). The NCLB included provision for Supplemental Education Services (SES) in public schools, public charter schools and other institutions (Mori, 2013, p. 195). Administrators in school districts with underperforming schools were required to allocate at least 20% of their federal "Title I" budget for supplementary tutoring, and to notify parents who were entitled to fee-free tutoring.

  Partnerships with tutoring providers had some significant achievements (Mori, 2013; Husband & Hunt, 2015), but also some problematic dimensions. Regulations had to be tightened after tutoring providers in New York, Michigan, Ohio and Florida were charged with falsification of student attendance records, bribing school officials and billing school authorities for tutoring that they had never provided (Santos, 2014). Washington State introduced further rules to forbid tutorial companies from knocking on doors to advertise and from approaching parents on school grounds while the parents were collecting or dropping off their children. The regulations also prohibited companies from telling parents that they would get free computers if they signed up for programmes, though still permitted giving such equipment after signing up if the equipment was used as part of the instructional programme; and after one school district alleged that three companies had submitted enrolment forms with forged signatures, parents were required to submit their own applications (Santos, 2014).

Linking to the point made above, advocacy of government support for tutoring proved effective in the context of the COVID-19 pandemic. In 2022, the federal authorities announced an American Rescue Plan (ARP) with US$122 billion "to combat learning loss" that had arisen during school closures. This included the launch of "the National Partnership for Student Success (NPSS) to provide students with an additional 250,000 tutors and mentors over the next three years" (The White House, 2022, p. 1).

The snapshots presented above are indicative of both a global trend and the complexities of issues, which have been accelerated and further complicated by the COVID-19 pandemic. Globalisation has facilitated the distribution of such policy discourse without thorough discussions of implications. Rather, as shown in the case of England, actors both in that country and in the USA could conveniently cite "evidence" from elsewhere to assert the necessity for public funding of nationwide tutoring schemes.

The government efforts listed in this section were mostly well-intended for closing financial and achievement gaps. However, some have unintentionally driven the expansion of tutoring, and/or in practice left out the target disadvantaged social groups. The "partnership" vocabulary has a positive orientation, but is not always smooth in operation and can have perverse effects in excessive marketisation, exacerbated social inequalities and legitimation of the tutoring industry. For these and related reasons, many governments have been cautious about public-private partnerships; and on their side, private entrepreneurs are sometimes wary of the bureaucratic constraints of collaboration with public bodies.

Notes

1 However, this picture changed dramatically with the introduction of tight regulations in 2021 – see Chapter 4.
2 In 2020, MEXT budgeted JPY7.37 billion, of which JPY6.74 billion was allocated to school-community partnership programmes for learning, JPY75 million to supporting family education, JPY47 million to supporting dropout students, JPY8 million for career counselling and planning and JPY99 million for experiential learning (Japan, 2020).

Part II
Five Country Studies

3 Japan
Changing Dynamics of Regulation and Self-Regulation

3.1 Origins and expansion of shadow education

Tutorial institutions in Japan are generally called *juku*. These institutions may be of many types, as pointed out by Roesgaard (2006) in her helpful typology and classification. For present purposes, the focus is on academic tutorial enterprises known as *gakushu juku*.

A *juku* historian (Sato, 2012) has documented the origins of these *gakushu juku* and associations of *juku* operators that support the industry. According to Sato (p. 145) the first *gakushu juku*, called Torimotojuku, was opened in 1912, and the first *juku* association was established in 1960. Torimotojuku was founded by a teacher in Tokyo who shifted from his school to this independent enterprise. He commenced by tutoring 10 Grade 6 students who were preparing for the selection process to lower secondary schooling. Most of the tutees gained admission to elite schools, and his reputation and enterprise grew.

Figures 3.1 and 3.2 show data on the expansion of *gakushu juku* institutions, employees and enrolments as recorded by the Ministry of Economy, Trade and Industry (METI) and the Ministry of Education, Culture, Sports, Science and Technology (MEXT). Other types of tutoring investigated by a national survey included private tutors and correspondence courses (Japan, MEXT, 2008). Tutoring participation rates of lower secondary students by private tutors declined from 5.4% in 1985 to 4.7% in 2007, while participation in correspondence courses increased from 11.8% in 1993 to 17.1% in 2007. The rates for primary students receiving help from private tutors were 1.0% in 1985 and 0.9% in 2007; and for correspondence courses they were 11.7% in 1993 and 19.5% in 2007 (Japan, MEXT, 2008, p. 9).

More recent data were provided by a 2015 national survey, which found that 47.7% of Grade 6 and 60.8% of Grade 9 students received tutoring in *gakushu juku* or with private tutors in Japanese, mathematics and

DOI: 10.4324/9781003318453-6

NUMBER OF GAKUSHU-JUKU AND EMPLOYEES

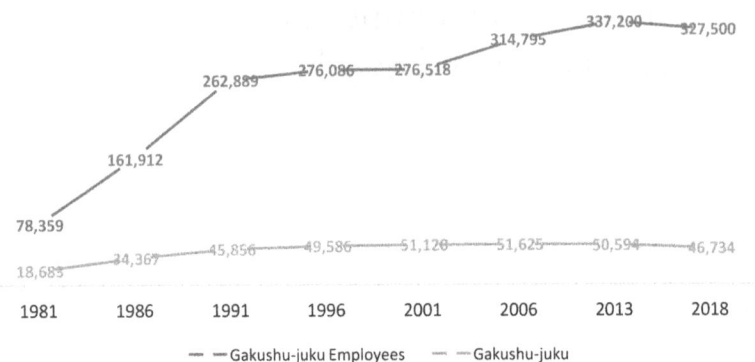

Figure 3.1 Expansion of Gakushu Juku, 1981–2018, Japan

Source: Japan (METI, 2013, 2019) and Sato (2012, p. 1039).

science (calculated from data in Japan, MEXT, 2015, p. 66). As tutoring for all levels expanded, the ages of children starting to receive tutoring became lower. Geographically, *juku* in the initial stage of development were concentrated in the capital metropolitan area; but by the 21st century, all provinces and municipalities had large numbers of *juku*.

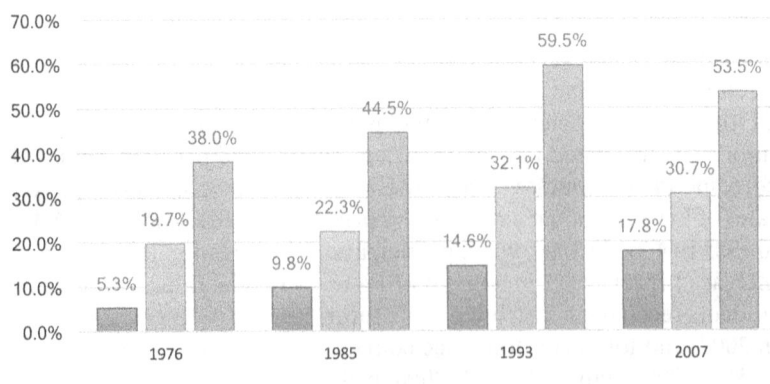

Figure 3.2 Changing Gakushu Juku Enrolment Rates by Level of Schooling, 1976–2007, Japan

Source: Japan (MEXT, 2008) and Sato (2012, p. 1034).

Japan   47

Many factors driving the expansion of shadow education resembled the drivers elsewhere. They included increased household incomes, expanded schooling at all levels, dominance of high-stakes examinations, and intensified credentialism and competition. Other factors were more specifically rooted in Japan's school system. They included unintentional consequences of school equalisation policies and curriculum reforms, with adverse effects such as gaps between school curriculum and lower- and upper-secondary entrance examinations.

Elaborating on the historical development, during the period up to World War II (WWII), schools and teachers were the dominant tutoring providers. Tutoring mostly took place in mainstream schools and focused on examination preparation for advancement to the next level of education. In 1929, MEXT issued a notice to prohibit primary schools from tutoring students for entrance examinations; and a 1937 notice emphasised the harmful impact of test preparation for primary students (Sato, 2012, p. 219). *Juku* were not visible during this period and were modest in scale. Some *juku* supported children, including ones from disadvantaged families, in the face of interrupted schooling during WWII. After WWII, *juku* multiplied because of growing demand and intensified competition for entrance to secondary education. Contextual factors included expanded school access (thus raising family aspirations for higher-level and elite schooling), stabilising economy, rising consumerism and sharply increased student numbers from the post-war baby boom.

Table 3.1 charts the post-WWII *juku* expansion to the 1990s. Among the unintentional drivers were policies devised for schooling. For example, in 1966 schools were prohibited from providing supplementary tutoring and examination (admission) preparation, despite the continuous increase in students desiring to advance to higher levels of education. Two years later, the 1968 national curriculum guidelines made school curricula more difficult and heavily loaded and led to a sharp increase in drop-outs. The 1966 policy left demand that used to be met by schools to the tutoring market; and the 1968 policy left drop-out students to *juku* specialised in such support. In a 1971 national survey, 65.4% of primary teachers and 80.4% of lower secondary teachers reported that students could not understand half the curriculum (Komiyama, 2012b, p. 282). As a result, the demand for remedial tutoring increased. *Juku* which specialised in helping students with school work were mostly established after this time.

Revisiting and learning from experience, 1977 guidelines set "relaxation" (*yutori*) as the principle to develop a new curriculum. Both curriculum content and academic learning time were reduced; yet parents felt that the curriculum reduction weakened the quality, and

Table 3.1 Juku Expansion and Evolution, Japan, Post-WWII to the 1990s

Stages of juku development	Social background of the times	Changes in mainstream education/ curriculum	Changes in juku, strategy, forms, modes of operation
"Germination"	**Post-WWII – 1960s** Rapid economic growth "standard deviation"; Stratification of schools + competition in high-school entrance exam	New education system post-WWII New curriculum implemented 1958 "systematic curricula" • Double-shift schooling continued • Curriculum focus on experience • Exam-oriented teaching at school	• Juku for private junior high school preparation founded in the 1950s • Juku are set up and run with founders' specific ideologies in education • One-person operation, small juku
"Growth"	**1960s** Nationwide standardised exam for junior high students conducted (1961–1966) Ranking of students and schools	• First baby-boom cohort enters middle school • 1968 new "meritocratic curriculum" • Heavy contents create many drop-outs • Supplemental classes at public schools active, then basically banned from 1966 • Parents become economically affluent • Parents expect higher education than before	• Private junior high school gained popularity in Tokyo and Kinki - primary school pupils receive private tutoring • Mainstream schools cannot cover all the material alone • Curriculum causes the need for tutoring

(Continued)

Table 3.1 Juku Expansion and Evolution, Japan, Post-WWII to the 1990s (Continued)

Stages of juku development	Social background of the times	Changes in mainstream education/curriculum	Changes in juku, strategy, forms, modes of operation
"Expansion"	**1970s** Oil shocks; Enterprises enter the juku industry as a promising field **1979** Introduction of Preliminary Standardised College Examination	• Drop-outs became a social problem • New curriculum, 1977 • Human-centred/Yutori curriculum	• Supplementary/prevention of drop-outs; juku increased • Enterprises opened franchise chain juku • Clear ranking of colleges, faculties
"Stabilisation"	**1980s** • Bullying in public middle schools pushed popularity of private schools • Younger age groups start attending juku	• New curriculum 1989; new learning ability • Diversified grading system introduced • Some juku founded mainstream private schools	• Demand for data and preparation for differentiated entrance exams to private schools
Minor amendments from MoE	**1990s**	• 1992: 5-days-a-week school system experiment	• MoE requested juku industry not to offer classes on Saturdays

Source: NIRA (National Institute for Research Advancement, 1996), presented in Yamato and Zhang (2017, p. 333).

the shortened hours of schooling released more time for tutoring. Moreover, the high-stakes examinations became more difficult even though the school curriculum was easier and lighter. The widening gap between school curriculum and entrance examinations drove more families to tutoring. Komiyama (2012a) analysed curriculum changes in English and mathematics. He found that the content and level of difficulty of English and mathematics textbooks was reduced enormously. Not only were the textbooks thinner, but many exercises and difficult questions had been deleted. However, examinations were not adjusted for consistency with the lighter curriculum. Rather, they went in the opposite direction, and high-stakes entrance examinations became increasingly difficult. Komiyama noted (2012a, p. 215) that: "Private high schools had the most difficult entrance examinations with questions that even college students would find challenging to solve". The widening gaps became a major driver of *juku* expansion from the 1970s onwards. As such, the curriculum reforms shifted from one end to the other, and unintentionally brought two booms to *juku*.

Other factors included the equalisation policy (see Zhang & Yamato, 2018) and reform of college entrance examinations (NIRA, 1996) that fuelled anxiety and insecurity and heated competition for elite schools and universities. Policies to improve equity included abolition of ability grouping, random assignment of students to public secondary schools, and rotation of teachers in public schools. These policies eroded confidence in public schooling, expanded competition for elite private schools, and fuelled demand for shadow education. Students had to prepare for entrance examinations by specific elite institutions, and also had to compete in national examinations following the 1979 establishment of a standardised system (NIRA, 1996, p. 12). Later reforms to diversify admissions just diversified the preparation needs (Box 3.1).

Box 3.1 Egalitarian rhetoric, meritocratic schooling and hierarchical society – the need for "double schooling"

Almost all *juku* practitioners interviewed by the author during her 2014–2019 fieldwork on public-private partnerships in tutoring held the view that schooling secured the baseline while tutoring nurtured diversity. Schools, this view implies, were for equalisation while *juku* were for differentiation.

Elaborating, many interviewees pointed out that schooling only provided basic learning in its official classes, though met the minimum learning needs for all and fostered all-round development in academic, moral, social, physical and artistic dimensions. Many parents felt that tutoring met additional and diverse learning needs unmet by schools, and especially remedial help, enrichment and accelerated learning. It seemed to be commonly accepted that examination preparation was the job of tutoring providers rather than schools. Some tutoring providers and parents even felt that *juku* liberated public schools from such preparation, allowing teachers not to teach to the test but to focus instead on all-round development.

Because one of the major foci of *juku* is the gap between high-stakes examinations and school curriculum, children without extra help were disadvantaged. Schooling that (only) met the basics meant that children who could not afford tutoring only got the basics. When schooling was a vital device for job allocation and social stratification, equal schooling for all simply meant a relatively equal fee-free starting point in a race where children without tutoring have to rely on their legs but those with tutoring ride bicycles. If children without tutoring are strong and diligent runners, they may be fast enough to compete for the limited quota to elite schools and universities, but the journey is tough. Likewise, the perception that remedial help should be met by tutors rather than teachers can discriminate against lower achievers. It implies that students with learning difficulties must either pay to catch up or find free help which should have been the school's responsibility.

Further nuances arise from the *juku* roles of guidance and in some cases backdoors to elite institutions. Dierkes (2011) pointed out that: "Given the role of *jukucho* [operators of small *juku*] in dispensing such advice, many private schools are increasingly courting *juku* operators through various kinds of fairs". Some *jukucho*, he added through varioor relationships with (predominantly private) schools that allow them not only to speak about some (somewhat local) schools with greater authority/inside knowledge, but potentially also to "get students into" these schools, even when their entrance examination result may have fallen slightly short of the result required. Similar partnerships between *juku* and private schools were found during the author's research (Zhang, 2018).

Even if Japan provides quality and equal education for all through public schooling, tutoring plays a significant role in the ostensibly meritocratic education system and in the highly hierarchical society. The government's achievements in quality and equity of schooling have to some extent been subverted by the shadow education system, and families to a large extent find that "double schooling" is required.

3.2 Changing official attitudes and regulatory approaches

Until a change of attitude at the turn of the century, MEXT had been dominated by the negative impact of tutoring and refused to recognise *juku*. The Constitution protected the free market and individual rights, which meant that *juku* could not be banned (Yuuki et al., 1987); and even during a so-called time of "*juku* chaos" in the 1970s (Sato, 2012, p. 258), MEXT kept its distance from the sector. Nevertheless, the 1980s brought initiatives by the Ministry of International Trade and Industry (MITI, which later became the Ministry of Economy, Trade and Industry – METI). In 1986, MITI started active promotion of *juku* self-regulation in response to complaints about contract cancellations, false advertising, and aggressive and/or malicious actions towards consumers (Ando, 2017). MITI held monthly meetings with a liaison committee from the tutoring industry to discuss matters, including the formation of a unified body to represent the industry that in 1987 produced a set of self-regulations. Standards set by these rules mainly focused on core areas of consumer disputes, including advertisement standards, active disclosure of information, the cooling-off rule and restrictions on sudden contract cancellations. In 1988, the Japan Juku Association (JJA) was established with MITI approval.

The fact that the JJA was endorsed by MITI for appropriate business conduct rather than by MEXT reflected the continuing MEXT denial of shadow education as part of the education system. In 2009, a Consumer Affairs Agency (CAA) was established and has also played a role in regulating tutoring (see Box 2.2). In addition to laws and regulations to protect consumers and promote fair competition, *juku* should also follow the Act on the Protection of Personal Information (Japan, 2003).

Yet from the 1970s onwards, MEXT was not entirely passive. MEXT was mindful of increasing criticism of *juku* for damaging students' holistic development, imposing financial burdens on families and damaging the morality of education. To alleviate the impact of tutoring on study load, competition and commodification, MEXT tried to steer it indirectly. MEXT monitored the overall shadow education situation through national surveys and sought to reduce demand by adjusting and improving public schooling. The first MEXT survey, in 1976, was entitled *Investigation into Out-of-School Learning for Students*. Subsequent nationwide surveys were conducted in 1985, 1993, 2002 and 2007, before being absorbed into broader modes of data collection. The surveys secured information on tutoring participation, expenditures and curriculum. They asked about parents' and students' attitudes towards tutoring, and analysed inequalities. Separately, data were collected through MEXT's biennial national household surveys. These surveys have a long tradition, and from 1994 onwards have included tutoring alongside other educational expenditures.

Other significant policies were issued in 1977 and 1987. The 1977 document from the Elementary and Secondary Education Bureau, entitled *Adjustment of Out-of-School Learning Activities for Students*, recognised that demand for *juku* was strongly related to the preparation for entrance examinations at all levels. Accordingly, the Ministry requested relevant parties to adjust entrance examinations in consideration of the students' study burden and the influence on schooling. Another attempt to educate consumers and *juku* operators was made in a 1987 Notification from the Administrative Vice-Minister entitled *Enhancement of Study Activities at School*. The document highlighted the negative impact of excessive *juku* participation, including burdens from activities during holidays and at night, and requested *juku* to address the situation (Isashiki, 2017).

As shadow education became entrenched in Japan, tutoring became a norm in many children's lives. MEXT realised that *juku* would not disappear despite the social criticism and official distancing, and that the market was supported by growing numbers of families. In 1999, the Lifelong Education Council (restructured in 2001 as the Subdivision on Lifelong Learning of the Central Council for Education) recognised the co-existence of *juku* and schooling, and the roles of tutoring in meeting differentiated family demand for what was not offered by schooling. This was in effect a form of official recognition of *juku* by MEXT as part of Japan's education system. Since then, MEXT has increasingly communicated and engaged with *juku* associations, and has tried to identify and harness their positive roles.

One reflection of MEXT's new approach was evident in management of its policy to abolish Saturday classes in schools. Three months before the five-days-per-week school system was implemented in 2002, MEXT's Lifelong Learning Policy Bureau visited the JJA for consultation and possible collaboration. MEXT was anxious for the *juku* operators to understand the new policies, and requested the JJA to dissuade its members from simply filling Saturdays with their own classes (Ando, 2017). The MEXT initiative was only partially successful but was nevertheless significant as a form of communication and potential partnership.

Further changes arose from two other pressures. First, both mainstream and shadow education suffered from declining birth rates in an ageing society; and second, international assessments of student performance pressed policy makers to identify ways to improve patterns.

MEXT increasingly viewed *juku* as important actors in the out-of-school learning space and tried to promote partnerships between schools, *juku* and communities. In 2014, a document entitled *Creation of Education Environment after School and on Saturday to Enrich Children's Learning* issued by the Subdivision on Lifelong Learning of the Central Council for Education officially recognised *juku* as partners in tutoring and experiential learning (Japan, MEXT, 2014). Since then, as mentioned in Chapter 2, tutoring providers have been increasingly visible and active in government-initiated *mirai juku* and other after-school programmes.

3.3 Bottom-up self-regulation

The expanded self-regulation evident in recent decades fits the vision set out in the 1988 establishment of the JJA, among the functions of which was setting "self-standards of appropriate business activities in the *juku* industry" (Isashiki, 2017). Among the foci for these self-standards have been contracts, disclosure of information, protection of consumers, protection of personal information, and assurance of children's health and safety. The JJA also certifies *juku* that meet standards, and monitors working conditions for part-time tutors.

Nevertheless, the JJA is only one of many *juku* associations, and its membership forms only 0.8% of the industry. Sato (2012) documented 50 major *juku* associations and noted that historically over 100 *juku* associations had existed, many of them small and localised. These associations bring together members of different categories, maintaining the diversity of the shadow education system. Some associations partner while others compete, depending on their missions. In addition to protecting their own members, some associations provide platforms for members to exchange experiences and conduct research in such areas as pedagogy and curriculum, tutor training, student recruitment, institutional management and business operations. These associations also strengthen the ability of *juku* to handle crises and risks. Small and quality *juku* have their own spaces to shine in their neighbourhoods, not being pushed out by aggressive big players. In addition to the Japanese culture of social trust that values reputation via word of mouth, the many *juku* associations play key protective roles in the ecosystem of shadow education.

Since the 1970s, various *juku* associations have collaborated in formal meetings. The first forum, in 1975, brought together over 50 representatives of national and regional associations to study basic laws in education, share research on textbooks, discuss the position of shadow education, and set educational goals (Sato, 2012, p. 259). The event was a milestone in the search for *juku* identity and legitimacy. Today the associations continue these roles, albeit with diversification and specialisation. Some of them organise regional and national mock examinations and rank students in ways that schools are forbidden to do. Families value these rankings as performance indicators when considering applications for elite schools and universities. Critics assert that these examinations and rankings perpetuate competition and stress, but advocates report that ironically they reduce the uncertainties and anxieties of at least some families.

3.4 Private-public partnerships

PPPs in shadow education emerged with the development of self-regulation. Although PPPs between tutoring and schooling were only officially established at the system level during the 2010s, partnerships between tutoring providers and both schools and local governments can be traced back to the 1960s. These partnerships expanded in a bottom-up manner despite the lack of official recognition by MEXT. Partnerships started with private-private collaboration between *juku* associations, *juku* and private schools, which expanded to PPPs with public schools and district education authorities. For example, in response to a management crisis, Gansai *Juku* Association sought guidance from policy makers and school leaders and then collaborated with schools for charity and volunteer services. *Juku* associations also supported the government to cope with disasters and other social crises. When private schools boomed, some local authorities even invited *juku* to open private schools.

In the contemporary era, therefore, all these forces mesh as depicted in Figure 3.3. The government and *juku* are working together, sometimes in passive *de facto* partnership and sometimes in active collaboration. Patterns may be complex in specific locations and in specific subject specialisations since they depend on the attitudes and skills of individuals as well as on the dynamics of particular communities. At the same time, the evolution over the decades is itself instructive and signals the likelihood of further collaboration and perhaps blurring of boundaries in the decades ahead.

PPPs initiated and subsidised by local governments and schools varied greatly. Problems associated with tutoring schemes subsidised by local governments included a bias towards large companies and lobbying by the *juku* associations. Despite regulations and stipulated transparency and fairness for bidding, the government seemed to

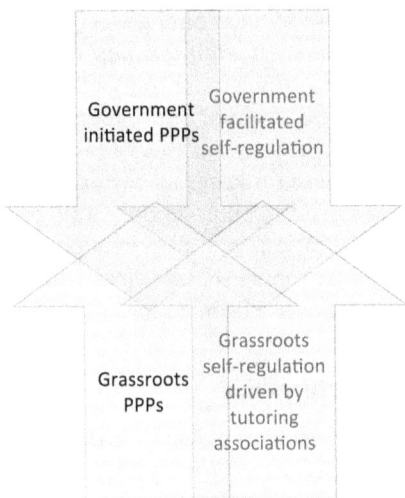

Figure 3.3 Juku Self-Regulation and Public-Private Partnerships in Japan

think that large companies had the reputations and better capacity to deliver and thus were more reliable. Some *juku* associations tried to mobilise their political power to adjust policies in favour of their members, and some such programmes were not monitored or evaluated properly. Case studies of summer tutoring courses conducted by the author in Tokyo showed that one was poorly coordinated and not evaluated, which reflected inefficient use of public funds and student time.

Schools also outsourced tutoring services to *juku*. Problems associated with such institutional initiatives included dependence on schools' social networks and lack of official regulations. Some private schools were criticised for hiring *juku* tutors to watch their students do homework, for which students had to pay high fees. However, the absence of fixed regulations was reported to offer flexibility and space for teachers and tutors to work together. Comparing partnerships with the local government and schools, one *juku* owner interviewed by the author noted:

> In the school-initiated tutoring programmes I am doing education, but in the government-funded programme I am doing a job. I am given the teaching materials and told how I should teach, and I do not have autonomy to use my own materials and teach in my way. I have to fill all sorts of forms to demonstrate that I am good. I have done well (for responsibility), but my performance should not be measured by what I write in the forms.

3.5 Summary

In terms of government regulations, the Japanese picture has been one of commercial rather than educational oversight. Self-regulation started with bottom-up initiatives relating to educational, commercial and social dimensions, and was reinforced by MITI engagement with the JJA on commercial dimensions. Later MEXT engaged in educational dimensions, including standards for tutors in conjunction with the JJA. MEXT monitored trends through national surveys, securing data on the scale, nature, modes, expenditures, drivers and impact of tutoring. Monitoring trends was a significant starting point for steering and regulating.

The Japanese experience also shows that school reforms can lead to unintended outcomes that subvert the policies. Equalisation in schools expanded tutoring as a mechanism to retain inequalities; and burden-reduction in schools expanded the burdens in tutoring classes. MEXT eventually realised that reforms in schooling required partnership and coordination with the shadow education sector. If MEXT had moved earlier, it would not have met such a strong and independent system operating on its own norms and rules.

This account of Japanese patterns highlights the emerging trends of partnerships in improving student achievements, supporting low-income students and promoting lifelong learning. However, PPPs have potential risks of legitimising tutoring in schools and of schools transferring part of their responsibilities. At the same time, changes in school reforms shaped promising trends in tutoring. The small *juku* have played and continue to play important social and educational roles, but many struggle to survive in face of declining birth rates.

4 China
Strong State Confronting Strong Market

In 2020, official sources estimated that half a million tutoring companies existed in China, almost equivalent to the total number of schools. Yet industrial actors who inspected open data on companies with training or tutoring as their business domains discovered over four million training institutions. Industrial research also reported the existence of over 11 million employees in the shadow education sector. These figures were contrasted to 537,100 schools and 18 million teachers in the mainstream system (China, Ministry of Education [MoE], 2020; Zhang & Bray, 2021).

A 2017 household survey by the China Institute for Educational Finance Research (Wei, 2018) showed that shadow education participation rates were highest in northeastern China, at 60.8%. The next highest were the eastern areas (38.1%), central areas (38.0%) and western areas (30.5%). Participation rates of urban students, at 44.8%, were more than double those of 21.8% of rural students. Average household annual expenditures on tutoring were RMB5,021 (US$724) per student nationwide. Urban China had not only higher enrolment rates but also higher per capita expenditures at RMB5,762 (US$831). Annual expenditures for rural students were only RMB1,580 (US$228). Other empirical studies showed that despite the expansion of shadow education, students from poorer families were generally excluded (Zhang & Bray, 2016; 2017; 2018). Until the enforcement of the "double [burden] reduction" policy in July 2021 (China, General Offices of the Communist Party of China Central Committee and the State Council, 2021), private tutoring had not only become a parallel system to schooling but in some respects overshadowed it.

Although private tutoring emerged in China only in the 1980s, its scale caught up with and surpassed levels in countries where shadow education had developed for a century. The expansion contributed to educational and socio-economic development but also brought

DOI: 10.4324/9781003318453-7

China 59

negative effects including subjecting families to vicious competition and pressurising students. China also used to lag far behind its neighbours in regulating tutoring, but within three years following the release of the first national policy on tutoring in 2018 became the country with the most detailed and comprehensive regulations enacted by the largest number of enforcement officials.

This chapter begins with a historical overview of shadow education, with attention to relationships between the school, the shadow and the family spaces. It then turns to the evolving regulation of shadow education. Finally, it presents major lessons in the initial enactment of China's 2021 policy.

4.1 Shadow education relationships with schools and families

During what may be called the pre-history between 1978 and 1989, shadow education in China was very modest in scale. The dominant agents for education were schools and families. Some free or low-fee tutoring was organised by schools for (i) intensive preparation for high-stakes examinations, and (ii) remedial classes for low achievers and enrichment classes for high achievers. Some scattered fee-charging tutoring was provided in homes, but very limited shadow education was evident in other spaces (Zhang & Bray, 2021).

Then *Stage 1* of development, 1990–1999, may be called the emergence and first boom. Shadow education expanded beyond schools and families, constituting a third learning space. Especially in cities, some teachers and school leaders utilised power in schools to secure clients for private tutoring delivered by themselves. Specialised tutoring centres began to emerge in significant numbers.

60 *Five Country Studies*

Stage 2, 2000–2010, may be called institutionalisation and the second boom. The government banned tutoring by schools, some of which moved their tutoring to company premises. Many self-employed tutors (including teacher-tutors) moved to tutoring institutions, which proliferated in commercial and residential premises. Many teachers and university students joined companies as part-time tutors, and online tutoring germinated in the virtual space.

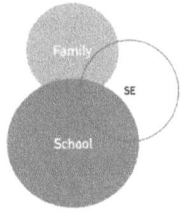

Stage 3, 2011–2018, was characterised by deepening institutionalisation, specialisation and capitalisation. Facilitated by EduTech advancement, traditional modes of tutoring were supplemented by online and dual-tutor formats with division of labour and specialisation in curriculum. Competition in the marketplace intensified, but entrepreneurs still had opportunities. The power of capital and development of professional tutors displaced teachers and schools in the tutoring marketplace. Major companies developed independent curricula that no longer followed schools, and the market took control of shadow education curricula and pedagogy in ways that challenged the official curriculum. Boundaries were blurred by public-private partnerships (see e.g. Zhang & Bray, 2017).

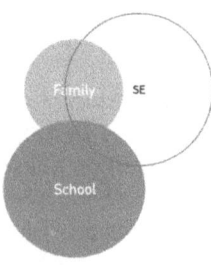

Stage 4, 2018–July 2021, was characterised by tougher government regulations introduced in 2018, and digitalisation and massification of tutoring fuelled by the COVID-19 outbreak. Despite the enforcement of national regulations on tutoring, major companies continued expansion in lower-tier cities and rural areas, utilising technological innovations. Online tutoring companies seized the opportunity to expand during the COVID-19 crisis. Technology companies such as

Baidu, Tencent and Bytedance expanded their shares in the online tutoring market by increasing investment and/or acquiring tutoring companies. Overseas capital flooded into the tutoring marketplace. Small companies were squeezed by large enterprises that were supported by venture capital and engaged in aggressive advertising. COVID-19 increased the power of technology and capital in digital learning, and online tutoring greatly expanded the shadow space.

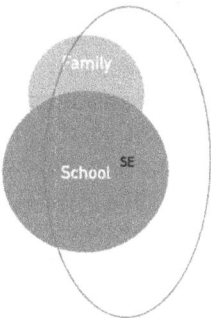

Stage 5, starting with the fierce regulations promulgated in July 2021, has been featured by legislation, decapitalisation and deindustrialisation. The strong state confronted the strong market with serious commitment. Laws and regulations were formulated at great speed, aspiring to "rectify" tutoring from "doing business" to "doing education", and to take the picture back to the pre-history era – or at least close to it – so as to retain the mainstream status of schooling. One immediate effect of the regulations was a sharp reduction in the scale of institutionalised tutoring and the rooting out of intensive capital. As such, the regulations had a striking impact on some symptoms and issues on the supply side. Yet many of the causes lay beyond shadow education and schooling, and much demand persisted that could not be fully met by schooling or family education. This demand was met through underground activities.

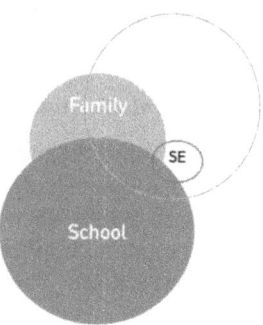

4.2 Regulating shadow education in and out of school

In its historical development, shadow education moved from the school space to the out-of-school marketplace. As the sector grew, some tutoring supplemented and supported schools and families, but some tutoring started to intrude on them. For over two decades, regulations mainly focused on (i) tutoring provided in schools by schools, and (ii) tutoring provided by teachers. These policies were issued in response to concerns about the heavy study burden and corruption risks.

To some extent, policies to reduce study burden, including the ban on low-fee tutoring organised by schools, unintentionally resulted in the expansion of tutoring in the private sector (Zhang & Bray, 2017; 2018). Also, the prohibition of teachers and schools from involvement in tutoring indirectly legitimised shadow education provided by private enterprises and self-employed tutors. Shadow education grew at great speed during the 2000s and 2010s, constituting a parallel system independent from schooling. However, it only attracted strong government attention in 2018, by which time it had been institutionalised as a norm in many (especially urban) families' daily lives.

Since 2018, the national government has been committed to regulating out-of-school tutoring run by private enterprises and individuals. The first phase was from 2018 until the COVID-19 outbreak when strong regulations were enforced to manage the commercial, social and educational dimensions of shadow education. Registered companies became more regulated, while unregistered (and therefore illegal) small-scale undertakings went underground. The COVID-19 outbreak led to the second phase of regulation featured by the closure of offline tutoring and a slightly relaxed environment for online tutoring. However, the aggressive expansion of online tutoring during the outbreak brought the national government to the realisation that shadow education had become a giant parallel system controlled by the market and threatening to overshadow and marginalise schooling. That led to the third phase of crackdown featured by deindustrialising and decapitalising shadow education.

4.2.1 Regulating tutoring by schools and teachers

To understand the picture more fully, it is useful to analyse the evolving regulation of shadow education during different historical periods. During the 1990s when tutoring emerged in a significant way, teachers were the main suppliers, operating independently or in conjunction with their schools. They were accompanied by informal suppliers such as college students, and by emerging tutorial institutions. The demand was stimulated by rapid expansion of post-primary schooling and accompanying expansion of opportunities for families able and willing to compete. The tutoring served both low and high achievers, and school-organised (and school-based) tutoring particularly focused on preparation for the *Zhongkao* (Grade 9) and *Gaokao* (Grade 12) examinations.

Other tutoring for elite students focused on Olympiad contests, particularly in mathematics, sciences and English. Regulations at the time mainly focused on tutoring provided by schools and on excessive training for Olympiads. For instance, a policy issued by the State Education Commission (SEC, renamed as Ministry of Education [MoE] in 1998) to reduce the study burden stipulated (China, SEC, 1994) that:

> after-school time and holidays should be used by the students freely and independently. Schools and teachers must not occupy students' free time. Nor should they organise school-based tutoring or use such time to teach new lessons (to accelerate instruction).

A year later, another national policy (China, SEC, 1995) prohibited schools from tutoring for Olympiads, or providing tutoring labelled "Advanced Class", "Gifted Class", or "Training Class". These policies unintentionally pushed teachers and schools away from school premises to tutoring in less visible sites and provided a market for other providers.

Further expansion of mainstream education during the 2000s, especially at the upper-secondary and post-secondary levels, drove even more demand for tutoring. Regulations in this period still focused on tutoring provision by schools and teachers. Some regulations were part of the burden-reduction policies that prohibited schools from accelerating instruction on the national curriculum and from providing tutoring (e.g. China, MoE, 2000; 2009). These regulations shortened official school hours and increased anxieties among some parents who then arranged tutoring to compensate (Zhang, 2014). The reduced school hours also released teachers' time for tutoring, and strengthened conspiracies between schools and tutoring companies. In 2005, another national policy prohibiting schools from training students for Olympiads (indicating the failure of the 1995 ban) created opportunities for tutoring companies to "take over" demand for such tutoring. To maintain their performance, some schools collaborated with companies by moving tutoring classes from their schools to partner companies or by sending students to companies with strong reputations for Olympiad tutoring. In 2008, a document on the Professional Ethics of Teachers stated that teachers "should reject paid tutoring with consciousness, and should not gain personal profit from their positions as teachers" (China, MoE, 2008, item 5). This was in response to teachers working as tutors and recommending students to other teachers and to tutoring companies.

Seven years later, a 2015 government document prohibiting schools and in-service teachers from providing tutoring (China, MoE, 2015) further delegitimised schools and teachers as tutoring suppliers. Tutoring institutions took over the market at great speed, accelerating its expansion by investing enormously in online tutoring. Major tutoring companies detached themselves from the schools, training their own professional tutors and developing independent curricula – some of which created challenges for schooling. When most students in school classes received tutoring, their teachers had to adjust the pace and content of classroom instruction to fit the tutoring curriculum. Some schools considered patterns advantageous when such tutoring boosted their students' academic performance, while other schools found it damaging when teachers were forced to accelerate school curricula to match the much more advanced pace of tutoring that was not necessarily suitable for the students' development. Some principals described it as schools being "kidnapped" by tutoring. Shadow education also increased students' study loads, depriving them of leisure after school hours on weekdays and at weekends. In addition, online tutoring was accused of damaging students' eyesight with excessive screen time.

4.2.2 Regulating tutoring by private enterprises

Concerned with these negative dimensions, in 2018 government policy shifted focus from mainstream providers to market players. An initial statement was jointly issued by four branches of the national government (China, People's Republic, 2018), and was followed a month later by a Ministry of Education notice to accelerate the regulation of tutoring enterprises (China, MoE, 2018). A third major document was issued in August 2018 by the General Office of the State Council with detailed instructions (China, GOSC, 2018), which reflected the national government's determination to regulate tutoring as a priority issue.

This document was the first national policy by the State Council about regulating private tutoring and marked the beginning of nationwide regulation of shadow education. Following the release of the policy, subnational regulations were formulated in line with requirements on registration (both business and educational licenses required), premises (safety and area), curriculum, curfew, tutor qualifications, fees and advertising (Zhang, 2019). Involvement of tutoring companies in school admissions and organisation of competitions and contests was also banned.

Recognising the importance of policy coordination on both shadow education and schooling, the document also included requirements for schooling. It reiterated the prohibition of teachers from providing tutoring and the prohibition of schools from collaborating with tutoring companies. It initiated after-school programmes (ASPs) for schools to absorb part of the demand for private tutoring, especially in terms of childcare and homework support. Institutionally, the policy set the framework for monitoring and supervision: the registration of tutoring institutions became subject to annual inspection and annual information disclosure, and a mechanism for dynamic blacklists and whitelists was established. Whitelists indicated registered companies compliant with the regulations and were publicised on the local government website, while institutions found to be violating the laws and regulations appeared on the blacklists. The lists changed according to the changing situation of compliance.

The main document was followed by a series of follow-up documents elaborating on requirements in specific domains. For instance, a document in November 2018 amended the measures for handling violations of professional ethics by primary and secondary school teachers. It specified punishment for teachers who organised or provided tutoring, and for teachers gained kickbacks from advertising tutoring or introducing students. Because much tutoring shifted from offline to online to circumvent regulations (such as the curfew and area per tutee), a national policy regulating online tutoring was released in July 2019 (China, MoE, 2019b).

The 2018 and 2019 measures had important implications for healthy and sustainable development not only of shadow education but also of schooling. The national government required efficient responses and timely feedback from local governments, which in turn provided experiences for refining national and local policies. The policy enactment raised awareness of both consumers and suppliers about aspects of safety and quality of shadow education. It was of great symbolic significance as "a knife hanging over the head" for tutoring providers that did not fall in line with the expected behavioural standards. The policy underlined that tutoring was an educational activity like schooling, and thus in many respects should be subject to the same moral standards. For consumers, the policy provided reminders of problematic dimensions and alerts of potential risks for example in fee refunds and in safety of children.

Enactment of the 2018–2019 policies resulted in a more regulated market which was most effective with the large tutoring enterprises (Zhang, 2019). It challenged the survival and legitimacy of medium-sized and small ones, among which some went underground. Enforcement of the policies involved considerable costs for both governments and tutoring companies. Tutoring companies invested much to obtain the licenses and comply, and many of them transferred the financial burden to consumers by raising prices.

At the same time, local governments experienced challenges from limited financial and human resources for enactment of the regulations. Some local education authorities took the lead in coordination and partnership between departments in enforcement, but ambiguities in responsibility led to prevarication. Other bodies such as the Fire Department and Public Security Bureau viewed responsibilities as lying with the education departments, so resisted extra work. For example in a second-tier city in southern China, an inspection team that discovered problems associated with fire safety had to wait a long time for the fire department to action since the education authority did not have relevant enforcement rights. In another city, the education authority received many complaints on refund disputes, falling under the enforcement power of the State Administration for Market Regulation (SAMR) which was short of law enforcement officers.

Further, although the system of dynamic blacklist and whitelist helped to guide consumers, rewarded compliant tutoring providers and disciplined non-compliant ones, arrangements could also be misleading (Box 4.1). Further, although the 2018 policy stipulated that tutoring institutions should not charge one-off fees for time spans exceeding three months, many providers still charged one-off fees for six months, a year or even two years. This practice allowed some unscrupulous businesses to roll up the money after receiving it. In response to such challenges, new regulations were devised to seek partnerships from banks.

4.2.3 COVID-19: Suspension of offline tutoring and tightening of financial regulations

During the COVID-19 outbreak in 2020, offline tutoring was suspended; and since online tutoring supported students' learning during the crisis, the government's attitude towards online tutoring softened.

> **Box 4.1 Side-effects from the dynamic blacklists and whitelists**
>
> Some blacklists in China did not specify the reason for blacklisting. Some companies on the list which had minor problems with facilities but not with the quality of tutoring or tutors were misunderstood by parents since they viewed blacklists as labels for poor quality of tutoring. This caused arguably unreasonable challenges for tutoring companies.
>
> By contrast, the whitelists caused challenges to consumers and governments. In 2019, a whitelisted tutoring company specialising in English (one of the largest, with over 200 chains in 60 cities across China) suddenly shut down. It absconded without due process, defaulting on the salaries of employees and preventing tutees either from attending classes or receiving fee refunds. Before the absconding, the company was already not paying wages but stepped up sales and induced tutees to purchase more courses. Worse still, it made students take loans if they could not afford immediate payments. Subsequent investigation indicated that the company was already suspected of fraud, and had conspired to take the tutees' money and then abscond. Many students were induced to subscribe for one or two years, against the regulations, because they trusted the company's reputation. It was estimated that several hundred million yuan were rolled away from the tutees. The incident damaged government credibility and made local authorities more cautious when whitelisting companies.

Government and school partnerships with online tutoring companies expanded. This indirectly sent signals to the market players, who saw great potential in online tutoring for huge profits.

These developments meant that online tutoring was dramatically boosted during 2020, accustoming millions of students to digital learning. The Key Laboratory of Big Data Mining and Knowledge Management (2020a, p. 17) reported that the online education consumer market grew from RMB8,520 (US$1,230) million in 2013 to RMB88,430 (US$12,780) million in 2020. The corresponding market penetration rate increased from 6.8% in 2013 to 15.0% in 2019, and jumped dramatically to 85.0% in early 2020 when COVID-19 struck. During this period, BigTech companies and capital flooded the marketplace, contributing to the wild expansion of online tutoring and to advertisement wars between the major players. Tens of billions were consumed by the advertisement arms race: big market players invested much more in advertisement than in curriculum development, teaching research and tutor professional development (see Box 4.2).

> **Box 4.2 Educational commitments marginalised by advertisement arms race, and educational goals marginalised by pursuit of profits**
>
> The market seized the opportunity of the COVID-19 pandemic to expand its control over education, threatening the power of the state and intruding into the autonomy of the family. Economic values overrode educational values, severely damaging the moral boundaries of the tutoring market. According to industrial analysis, the tutoring industry accounted for 6% of the number of advertisements by key industries in 2020, ranking fourth in the number of advertisements by key industries. Ten tutoring institutions spent more than RMB10 billion on marketing within just the two months of summer vacation. Tutoring advertisements were dominant in official television and the most popular variety shows.
>
> As an example, the financial report of Gaotu TechEdu for the third quarter of 2020 indicated that its sales and marketing expenses were RMB2.056 billion, 9.3 times higher than its research and development expenses of RMB220 million. The marketing arms-race not only brought extremely rapid growth in advertising but also false advertising and unfair competition. Amidst the chaos, small and medium-sized institutions that could not afford to burn money were gradually pushed out.
>
> In addition to faking the effectiveness of tutoring and the qualifications of tutors, the advertisements exaggerated the severity of competition in the education system, exacerbated anxieties and advocated twisted values. A quote widely criticised by the media was: "If you come to our centre, we will support your child; if you don't come to our centre, we will support [create] your child's competitors". Other advertisements created parental guilt. A video clip on a popular platform advertising a major online tutoring company presented a fake story of three students in front of the release board of *Gaokao* (Grade 12 examination) results. Two students were excited that they had been admitted to the top universities, and attributed the achievement to the company. The third did not make it, even though her score was high, and blamed her mother for not investing in tutoring from the company. The advertisement seemed to ascribe failure to enter the top universities to a lack of tutoring and hinted that parents who did not secure tutoring were irresponsible.
>
> These patterns reflected broader forces, with economic rationality and instrumentalism replacing educational rationality in both supply and demand. On the supply side, entrepreneurs exploited commercial interests; and on the demand side, many parents sought value for money. Both sides overlooked fundamental values and the wider aspects of learning in educational processes. The intrusion of capital

and technology also changed balances in the internal ecosystems of shadow education, resulting in many small institutions of high quality losing the space needed to survive.

Shadow education could be a laboratory for educational explorations, and in turn, become a potential driving force for school transformation. Indeed, numerous beneficial strategies and innovations had been made by online tutoring providers in terms of tools and modes during and before the COVID-19 pandemic. However, the technical means were mainly used to replicate offline scenarios and promote large-scale production, which, in combination with other factors, resulted in much content homogeneity. Problems of data and privacy infringement also worsened.

At the same time, many offline tutoring centres collapsed during the outbreak, and some online tutoring companies lost clients as the competition intensified. Take-the-money-and-run cases increased sharply in 2020 and 2021. Regulators in Shanghai took the lead in regulations on the finances of tutoring companies, and others followed. In Tianjin, for example, regulations specified the maximum amounts of daily and weekly expenditure from the accounts set up by tutoring companies in stipulated banks for receiving tutoring fees and instructed the banks to report unusual cash flow.

The national government also took action in response to rising consumer complaints. In October 2020, the MoE and SAMR issued a joint document to initiate a nationwide focused rectification against the illegal acts of tutoring institutions. They highlighted unfair contract clauses that infringed consumer rights and interests, "in order to regulate the contractual behaviour of tutoring institutions, resolve disputes over tutoring contracts effectively, and safeguard the legitimate rights and interests of consumers" (China, MoE and SAMR, 2020).

As such, long-existing problems were exacerbated, including false advertisement, unfair competition, consumer rights violation and low-quality tutoring. The national government had tackled these problems in 2018 and 2019 with some success. However, the policy makers found that once shadow education became a favourite target for national and international capital investment, it operated – perhaps even more than in the other countries addressed by this book – like a wild horse running at a speed that moderate regulations could not slow. In addition, concerns intensified on the larger issues of capitalisation and industrialisation of shadow education, which had become a stand-alone system with backwash on school operations.

4.3 Reclaiming the status of mainstream schooling

As a result of the patterns described, in July 2021 the Communist Party of China Central Committee and the State Council jointly released a policy entitled "Further Reducing the Burden of Homework and Out-of-school Tutoring for Compulsory Education Students" (China, General Offices of the Communist Party of China Central Committee and the State Council, 2021). The policy aimed at "double reduction", i.e. of study burden from schooling and from external tutoring. The overall goals were to protect student well-being, reduce the study and financial burdens, and alleviate parental anxieties. The measures on tutoring specifically targeted the for-profit nature of capital, which was viewed as the cause of many negative aspects of the industry. The overall policy was followed by a series of regulations addressing specific aspects, such as tutoring materials, fees, advertising, contracts and tutors' qualifications.

While the 2018–2019 policies emphasised regulating the development of the tutoring industry, the 2021 policy measures particularly aimed to deindustrialise and decapitalise it, in the process reducing the size of the market and returning the students' centre of gravity to their schools. It was a positional strategy to safeguard schooling, and a more comprehensive agenda to improve education for equity and student wellbeing.

At the level of compulsory education, academic tutoring providers were required to become not-for-profit institutions. While these providers previously had most of their business during summer and winter holidays and weekends, these slots were now prohibited, with academic tutoring being restricted to evenings on working days. Accompanying measures addressed public schooling, and the government collaborated with the media and schools to promote rational consumption and parental responsibility. After-school programmes were developed, and the school day at the compulsory education level was lengthened by extended education (which usually lasted from 3.30 pm to 5.00–6.30 pm for primary students, and from 4.30–5.30 pm to 6.30–8.30 pm for lower secondary students, varying by region).

Most of these measures focused on the supply of education. The official discourse was clear that schools should be the principal institutions fulfilling educational goals. Schools, the discourse added, should not push the responsibilities to families and shadow education and should provide equitable and quality education for all. In this perspective, shadow education should be very limited and no more than a complement to schooling when necessary.

On the demand side, after-school programmes did absorb some childcare needs and provide homework support that had previously been offered by the tutoring providers. Some parents who had been forced to arrange tutoring under peer pressure or because their children could not catch up in class when most others were receiving tutoring felt relieved that they could relax a little. Many such parents started rearranging their children's timetables and reflected on the problems brought by intensive parenting, though they were uncertain how long the honeymoon period would last until they were again confronted by the pressures of high-stakes examinations. Some immediately became anxious when they discovered that other parents were not slowing down in the way that they had done.

Adding numerical analysis, the China Education Panel Survey compared patterns before and after the double-burden-reduction policy. It showed a decline in the tutoring participation rate (Wang, 2021). In the 2021 spring semester, 48.1% of primary and lower secondary students had received (academic) tutoring, and the figure dropped to 21.7% in the fall semester. Participation rates in non-academic tutoring and home tutoring also dropped – from 50.8% to 38.9%. However, the data had ambiguities, including that home tutoring (i.e. hiring home tutors) was not separated from non-academic tutoring, even though much home tutoring was academic. Another study showed that one-third of parents still considered shadow education necessary and anticipated continuing with it despite the ban (Zhang, 2021a). Many middle-class parents in large cities became more anxious as a result of the policy since the competition remained fierce for their children but they had fewer choices in the marketplace.

Related, the policy had an immediate impact on the shadow education providers, especially in the capital market, and on other registered tutoring companies. Four months after its implementation, the industry had seen a sharp drawback in capital investment. The companies that had been among the largest in the world listed in the stock market had to cut out their academic tutoring, and some companies went bankrupt. An estimated 60–80% of employees in these tutoring companies were expected to lose their jobs. However, many turned to hidden self-employment online or offline.

These hidden activities signalled that while the legitimate tutoring companies suffered from fierce regulations, the black market expanded in response to the persistent demand. Self-employed tutors and informal classes mushroomed, and parents with social and financial capital formed "learning pods" for group tutoring. The government released regulations in response, and sample contracts reminded parents of the potential risks of illegal tutoring. However, as long as parents still felt that schooling was not enough to give their children the learning they expected (such as personalised attention), and felt pressed by the continued competition in the stratified system, such demand for tutoring would not disappear.

The policy has yielded complex implications for equity. Families that previously had little access to tutoring generally felt that it showed a strong commitment to equality. At the other end of the scale, the privileged social elites who could arrange private tutors rather than being dependent on the companies were little affected. Among the lower-middle- and middle-middle-class families, many felt that the policy made life more difficult: they previously had many choices in the marketplace and could compare prices and choose affordable tutoring services. Now they had either to reduce tutoring, leaving their children's fate mostly to schools, or to risk using tutoring in the black market full of uncertainties in terms of quality, safety and price. For the government, the expanding black market was much more challenging to regulate than the registered institutions.

4.4 Extending analysis of the double-reduction measures

The double-reduction policy demonstrated learning as portrayed in the general regulatory framework presented in Chapter 1 (Figure 1.2), and permits extension of the framework.

4.4.1 Concerted policy enactment with attention to schooling, shadow education and family education

Recognising that the school, family and shadow education spaces are all integral parts for educating the young generation, the 2021 policies devoted concerted efforts to both schooling and shadow education with additional attention to family education. On the one hand, the measures tried to reduce the scale of tutoring and crack down on harmful practices. On the other hand, they tried to safeguard schools from the backwash of tutoring, to reinforce school responsibilities, and to strengthen the quality and equity of schooling. Additionally, a policy to promote family education was issued to reinforce the parental role as the first educators of their children and the space of family as the first classroom for children (Xinhua, 2021).

The double-reduction policy and accompanying actions tried to tackle both the symptoms and the causes of the challenges. The measures to drive capital out of education in academic subjects at the compulsory level were very effective. In addition to the not-for-profit requirement and ban on tutoring during weekends and holidays, companies were prohibited from raising capital on stock exchanges.

When the supply of tutoring was reduced and regulated, After-School Programmes (ASPs) developed at great speed in schools to absorb some of the demand that used to be met by tutoring, such as child care, extracurricular activities and homework support. New ASPs were developed and offered nationwide within just three months of the double-reduction policy, albeit with disparities in quality around the country. ASPs were welcomed by many parents but also increased the burdens on schools and teachers. Local governments sought creative ways to channel quality education resources from providers of non-academic tutoring to serve ASPs in schools. Aggressive advertisements which used to flood almost all public areas disappeared. Yet despite this progress, the fundamental causes of social culture and competition took much longer to address.

4.4.2 Institutional transformation to secure human and financial resources

Qualified personnel were needed at the local levels of government not just for regulation and site checks, but also for checking the tutoring materials which needed experts on curriculum and textbooks. The local governments also had to secure funding and technical support for digital governance as a way to compensate for lack of qualified personnel. Most importantly, institutional transformation was required to establish enforcement mechanisms.

Prevarication was a major obstacle to enactment. Yet, learning from previous experiences, a department for regulating tutoring was established in the Ministry of Education a month before the release of the double-reduction policy. Corresponding departments were established at provincial, municipal and district levels, and these authorities were granted greater enforcement rights to regulate shadow education.

Due to the importance of the double-reduction policy, various departments in the central government independently took serious action. Most tutoring regulations before the double reduction were issued by the Ministry of Education, sometimes in partnership with other Ministries. After the announcement of the double-reduction policy, all relevant departments issued regulations independently or took the lead to show their commitment and determination. The action at the national level pressurised corresponding departments at the local level to respond rapidly and efficiently. For instance, the

Ministry of Civil Affairs oversaw the registration of tutoring institutions, the State Administration for Market Regulation took the lead in regulating advertisements, and the National Development and Reform Commission took the lead in regulating and monitoring tutoring fees (China, National Development and Reform Commission, 2021). Partnership and coordination between departments and divisions within education authorities improved because of a clear division of labour and strong signals from the central government. However, as different departments competed to show their contributions to regulating tutoring, tutoring providers encountered more fierce rectification from diverse departments.

4.4.3 Partnerships, educating the consumers and self-regulation

In addition to partnerships with schools in ASPs, and partnerships within the government, three other domains saw strong and effective partnerships:

- *Partnerships with the media* were strengthened for advocacy and educating the consumers. Efforts by the official media prior to the release of the policy helped to set the stage, preparing the public and tutoring providers for what was to come. Shadow education had already received much media criticism, and the initiatives led to another wave of advocacy for tighter regulation. The media also helped to make the policies comprehensible to both suppliers and consumers. Experts were invited to write their views and interpretations of each policy document for the Ministry websites and attracted further media attention.
- *Partnerships with research institutions* such as universities and think tanks were strengthened for policy evaluation and refinement, and for supporting self-regulation. The government funded research institutions to monitor risks, evaluate progress, summarise public opinions and support evidence-based policy refinement. The institutions also initiated such research independently, and submitted policy papers to shape the decision-making.

The top-down and bottom-up policy consultation framework allowed timely feedback for policy refinement. It contributed to a learning(changing)-as-you-go model of policy enactment, in which policy makers could secure feedback and adjust with great flexibility. For instance, the standards for defining academic and non-academic tutoring (of which the latter was core for regulating tutoring since academic tutoring was under much harsher regulations than non-academic tutoring) first released by the Ministry of Education caused confusion and ambiguities for enactment. In collaboration with the Shanghai Municipal Education Commission (SMEC), the Centre for International Research in Supplementary Tutoring (CIRIST) at East China Normal University (ECNU) conducted related research and organised an expert committee with colleagues in the ECNU Institute of Curriculum and Instruction (ICI) to devise more professional and feasible principles for classification. CIRIST also established an expert evaluation platform and a dynamic database for typical cases in partnership with Shanghai Tutoring Association (STA). The initiative received positive feedback from the industry and parents, and other cities followed. The model later became part of the national policy and was implemented nationwide.

Shanghai was also innovative in its use of professional and scholarly bodies to support bottom-up self-regulation. The government encouraged the establishment of the STA in 2020 as an independent professional association. It was a not-for-profit independent legal entity jointly initiated by ECNU, Shanghai Open University, Shanghai Centre for Teacher Training, Shanghai Association for Education Evaluation, tutoring companies and other public education institutions. Before the foundation of the STA, self-regulation was mostly led by official not-for-profit professional associations (Zhang, 2019). However, these bodies focused on wider private education and represented a top-down approach to self-regulation.

Another type of body that claimed a professional identity brought together a significant number of small and medium-sized enterprises (Zhang, 2019). These were for-profit bodies and thus more commercial. They publicly supported government regulations but provided coping strategies for the enterprises to circumvent regulations. They made a profit mainly by providing business consultations and training, with little attention to the professional development of tutoring providers as educators. These bodies were not recognised by the government as official associations and were controversial for their grey-area practices.

The STA had a new model insofar as it was the first tutoring association for bottom-up self-regulation, with leadership and guidance from educational researchers and professionals. It played a more neutral role with greater independence from the government and the industry.

- *Partnerships with banks and other financial institutions* were established nationwide to regulate the finances of tutoring institutions. One focus was on charging of fees in advance, in response to the increasing number of tutoring enterprises absconding with money. Under the regulation, all advance charges were to be entered into designated accounts for which the banks would not charge additional fees. The tutorial companies were then required to designate proportions of the deposits as financial guarantees for fulfilling their commitments. Specific details were set by the local authorities around the country. Banks were also instructed not to provide loans to parents seeking to use the finance to pay tutoring fees and were required to strengthen the supervision of their loans directly to the tutoring sector.

4.5 Summary

The double-reduction policy and the accompanying measures were an evolving policy movement. Behind the measures was a learning government with persistence and commitment. National and local authorities were efficient and flexible to learn and adjust. The fast-moving adjustments were important for policy improvement but also caused challenges to those regulating and those regulated. This is a long-existing feature of the Chinese context. There is a popular saying about policy enactment in China: "Whenever there is a measure, there is a counter-measure". But that is only half of the story. The other half is best put as: "Whenever there is a counter-measure, there is a (re-)measure".

In learning, adjusting and trying, China is feeling its way in the longstanding challenge of balancing regulation and relaxation, and in finding appropriate levels of state intervention. In the process, the education professional power has played an important role in mediating conflicts and tensions between the state and the market.

The Chinese experience shows the usefulness of the general policy framework set out in Chapter 1 (Figure 1.2). The official national initiative to regulate tutoring started only in 2018, but policy makers mobilised think tanks to learn rapidly from other countries and adapted lessons to the local context. The policy on shadow education since 2018 reflects the five dimensions in Figure 1.2 and generated contextually rich experiences including:

- *Ongoing national commitment* to regulate the sector, to coordinate, guide and support local authorities in enactment, and to extract and share experiences to reduce regional disparities in regulatory capacity.

- *Institutional transformation* to secure allocation of qualified human resources and sufficient financial resources, and availability of technological means for enforcement.
- *Reflectivity* in policy enactment by mobilising education specialists and other professionals: soliciting opinions from various stakeholders and active learning from experiences to adjust policy text and practice.
- *Partnerships* within the government (cross-regional and cross-departmental), and with the media, banks, think tanks, education specialists, and schools.
- *Concerted policy making* with holistic planning of schooling, shadow education and family education.

The Chinese authorities have been chasing a fast-changing system. Serious national regulation was introduced only when the shadow sector had grown for over two decades and had become larger than the school system in terms of the number of institutions and staff. Partly as a result, the cost of regulation (resource and time) was high. Many tutors lost their jobs and many others moved to, or remained, in the grey market. These self-employed tutors were difficult to trace.

The experience also showed that online tutoring cannot be regulated effectively if only focused on tutoring providers. Venture investors and technology companies are aggressive driving forces. Yet this requires balancing the state and the market. Thus, too much top-down regulation could result in insufficient support for bottom-up self-regulation of companies and associations. Some sub-national governments, including that in Shanghai, learned to move towards professional bottom-up self-regulation.

Balancing continuity and change, the learning-as-you-go policy model could be flexible and adaptive but could cause confusion and reduce willingness to comply. Related was the danger of "whack-a-mole" policies: before devising new policies to address the symptoms, policy makers needed to listen more to the industrial voices and base policy adjustments on comprehensive understanding of the causes for their counter-measures. Only by doing so can authorities avoid falling into the trap of *ad hoc* arrangements.

Finally, China's double-reduction movement is a unique example of a strong state confronting a strong market in the domain of private tutoring. Rather than lip service to critique the negative dimensions of privatisation and marketisation in education, the Chinese government took action. The determination and huge effort devoted to regulating tutoring at national and local levels were to be applauded. Yet, as the society develops and expectations for education expand and diversify, schools alone cannot fulfil all educational goals and solve all social problems, especially when they are caught in the tensions between private and public goods. As shown by comparative studies (e.g. Christensen & Zhang, 2021; Zhang, 2021b), the root of shadow education problems in China lies not just in education but also in the wider society. Parental anxieties may appear to be educational anxieties, but they reflect status anxieties and social construction of achievement and success in a hierarchical society of deepening social stratification and accelerating change.

5 India
Diversity in a Decentralised System

5.1 Moving from the periphery to national government attention

Majumdar (2018, p. 274) quoted newspaper advertisements in Calcutta (present-day Kolkata) from upper-class households seeking private tutors in the 1890s, thus indicating that the phenomenon has a long history. During the 20th century both one-to-one tutoring and coaching classes became common across social groups. Thus, for example, Kale (1970, p. 375), writing about a city in Maharashtra, indicated that (p. 375):

> Many of the coaching classes ... which began as moon-lighting or independent entrepreneurial activity of gifted teachers have turned into large organizations. The hordes of students preparing for the statewide [Secondary School Certificate] examinations create a demand for their services. The tuition or coaching class teacher tries to give the student an effective examination technique, based mostly on memorization of ready-made answers.

One of Kale's interviewees remarked (p. 375), with a statement that still resonates in the contemporary era, that:

> Teaching in recent years has been commercialized. Teachers earn five times more money from tutoring than from regular salary. They have turned teaching into a business – a corrupt business. Why do they do that? Because they have no security. The society expects the school master to be a missionary but does not give him the security, income, insurance, pension that he needs.

By stages the phenomenon entered official agendas, though slowly. The 1986 *National Policy on Education* (India, Ministry of Human

DOI: 10.4324/9781003318453-8

Resource Development, 1986) did not mention the matter. Task forces leading to revision of the National Policy in 1992 did mention coaching, mostly approvingly as a mechanism to provide remedial support and reduce social inequalities. Less positively, the combined report from the task forces (India, Ministry of Human Resource Development, 1992, p. 75) referred to "instances of teachers conducting themselves in a manner not befitting the profession", including "requiring students to do unnecessary chores and inducing pupils to take private tuitions". However, the matter was not incorporated into the 1992 revision of the National Policy.

The theme came more strongly to the fore in association with discussions about the Right to Education (RTE) Act, which was passed in 2009. The Act provides for free and compulsory education to all children aged six to 14, and includes the stipulation (India, Ministry of Law and Justice, 2009, Article 28) that "No teacher shall engage himself or herself in private tuition or private teaching activity". Further, the 2020 *National Education Policy* that replaced the 1986/1992 predecessor mentioned coaching seven times. It contained a section (India, Ministry of Human Resource Development, 2020, p. 29) headed "Stopping commercialisation of education", and indicated intent to reduce coaching by promoting formative rather than summative assessment. Specifically, it stated (para 4.32) that:

> The current nature of secondary school exams, including Board exams and entrance exams – and the resulting coaching culture of today – are doing much harm, especially at the secondary school level, replacing valuable time for true learning with excessive exam coaching and preparation.

Nevertheless, India has a complex system of governance in which sub-national levels also play major roles. The country has 28 states and eight union territories. Education is on the concurrent list, meaning that both national and state governments can legislate on the subject. The national government is expected to set overall directions while state governments proceed with more specific priorities according to their contexts. Within individual states, further diversity arises from the perspectives and actions at district and lower levels.

5.2 The scale of private tutoring

Awareness and accompanying analysis of private tutoring in India have been improved by inclusion of the topic in official public expenditure surveys. Tables 5.1 and 5.2 present data from the household survey

Table 5.1 Enrolment Rates in Private Tutoring, by Level of Education, India, 2017/18 (%)

Level	Rural	Urban	Total
Pre-primary	9.2	15.6	11.6
Primary	13.7	24.6	16.4
Upper primary/middle	19.4	29.4	21.9
Secondary	27.2	38.3	30.2
Higher secondary	23.1	36.8	27.5

Source: India, National Statistical Office (2020, p. 113).

conducted by the National Statistical Office in 2017/18. The report presented these data under the heading of "coaching", but included what might also be called tuition (or tutoring). For the household survey, coaching was defined as instruction "taken by a student individually or in a group, at home or in any other place, by a single or more tutors" (India, National Statistical Office, 2020, p. 16). The statistics indicated that nearly one-third of secondary and higher secondary students were receiving coaching, and that even at the pre-primary level 11.6% of children were doing so. Proportions were significantly higher in urban than rural areas.

Even more striking were variations by state and union territory as shown in Table 5.2. The range in enrolment rates was huge. At the

Table 5.2 Enrolment Rates in Private Tutoring, by State/Union Territory, India, 2017/18 (%)

State	Rural	Urban	Total	State	Rural	Urban	Total
Andhra Pradesh	4.7	6.9	5.5	Kerala	16.7	20.2	18.3
Assam	21.2	37.1	22.9	Madhya Pradesh	6.7	24.9	11.5
Bihar	36.7	41.8	37.3	Maharashtra	7.0	32.7	18.2
Chhattisgarh	2.0	14.9	4.3	Odisha	40.4	52.6	42.5
Delhi	-	33.2	32.7	Punjab	12.3	19.6	14.8
Gujarat	5.2	28.8	14.3	Rajasthan	2.0	10.4	4.0
Haryana	6.6	19.3	10.8	Tamil Nadu	4.1	12.4	8.0
Himachal Pradesh	3.5	11.6	4.4	Telangana	0.5	4.3	2.3
Jammu & Kashmir	14.3	28.5	17.4	Uttarakhand	12.1	20.4	14.2
Jharkhand	22.8	43.5	27.0	Uttar Pradesh	8.3	22.3	11.2
Karnataka	2.8	7.9	4.7	West Bengal	74.3	77.8	75.2
				All India	17.3	26.0	19.8

Note: Some states and union territories were omitted.
Source: India, National Statistical Office (2020, p. 185).

top end were West Bengal and Odisha at 75.2% and 42.5%, respectively, while at the bottom were Telangana at 2.3% and Rajasthan at 4.0%. Marked differences were again evident between urban and rural areas.

5.3 Regulating the sector

Concerning regulation for private tutoring, complexities arise from India's federal system. At the national level, the Companies Act sets a general framework for businesses of all kinds (India, Ministry of Corporate Affairs 2013). More specific regulations have been devised by some state governments, while others have taken a *laissez faire* approach.

Among the early movers for specific regulations was Maharashtra. Bhorkar (2021) reported that the 1948 Bombay Shops and Establishments Act had long provided a general framework. In 2000, the Maharashtra Coaching Classes (Regulation) Ordinance laid out more specific rules regarding registration procedures. However, both these laws merely specified registration requirements and procedures, and, Bhorkar indicated (p. 30), "with no retribution laid out for offenders, neither of the laws seems to have been strictly implemented". In 2014 a newly appointed Minister tackled the issues, highlighting poor quality of instruction, inability of students to withdraw because of prepaid exorbitant fees, unsafe and cramped classrooms and distorted advertisements. He commissioned drafting of a new Act, but objections by members of tutoring associations altered or removed many provisions and reducing the draft to continued focus only on registration, infrastructure and taxation. In the event, even this version had not been approved by the legislature by 2019 when the Minister who had embarked on the reforms concluded his period in office and a new regime took over (Bhorkar, 2021, p. 256).

Another early mover was the government of Goa, which promulgated regulations in 2001 (Goa, 2001). Like Maharashtra, it required the operators of coaching classes to undertake initial registration. It also required renewal on an annual basis, and prohibited employment of tutors who were currently employed by any government-funded institution. Operators were also prohibited from using the premises of government-funded institutions.

Comparable in coverage were provisions in Uttar Pradesh in 2002 (Uttar Pradesh, 2002a; 2002b), but with registrations valid for three years and with other variations. They were followed by Bihar eight years later (Bihar, 2010) where, as in Uttar Pradesh, registrations were valid for three years. The Bihar regulations also stipulated minimum space of one square metre per student, together with "sufficient" furniture, lighting, toilets and other provisions of infrastructure. The wording from Bihar was largely duplicated in Manipur and Odisha seven years later (Odisha, 2017; Manipur, 2017). In Tripura, regulations were more specifically linked to the 2009 Right to Education Act. In 2011 the state government issued a ban on private tutoring by government teachers, which was followed up in 2015 by a High Court order. This order reinforced the ban on private tutoring by government-employed teachers, but did permit private teachers to provide tutoring for students over the age of 14 – that being beyond the age for free and compulsory education designated by the RTE Act – provided the students were registered in schools other than their own (Bhattacharjee, 2015; Barman, 2020).

In many cases, these regulations were introduced in response to immediate pressures, but they were not always enacted effectively. Thus in Bihar, for example, the Minister of Education was reported in 2017 to have indicated that to date 978 institutes had applied for registration but only 233 had actually been registered (Kumar, 2017). Further, the minister recognised, 2,000 to 2,500 large and small coaching institutes were operating in the state capital, and many more would have been operating in other parts of the state. The gap between declared intent and implemented reality reflected constraints in the machinery within competing priorities. In Tripura, competing forces were evident not only in the unwillingness of teachers to abandon tutoring but also in the desires of at least some parents to remain able to access the services (Box 5.1).

Box 5.1 Parental dismay at tutoring prohibition in Tripura State, India

In 2015 Tripura's High Court banned provision of private tutoring by government teachers. Teachers in private schools were permitted to continue, but only for children over the age of 14.

This ban caused protests from various student and parental pressure groups. As reported by *The Times of India* (2015), the convenor of one group argued that: "The students at the secondary and higher secondary levels are facing tough competition in various entrance tests", and that "unless they get extra coaching, it is impossible for them to pass those exams". The convenor added that most teachers had already

> stopped providing tutoring following the Court's move, with the result that "many students became demoralized".
>
> Despite such representations, the government held firm. However, some tutoring continued, leading to a repeat Ministerial prohibition in 2020. Again this led to protests that without private tutoring, students could not perform well in competitive examinations. One spokesperson (reported by *TripuraInfo*, 2020) declared that: "In actual classes in schools it is impossible for teachers to clarify everything within the limited time or periods; the syllabus for classes XI and XII is huge and without private tuition by teachers of schools ... students cannot even finish the syllabus for board exams, let alone prepare well for [the more prestigious] competitive exams".
>
> The spokesperson added that: "A government should go by the reality of the situation and not by illogical thinking; our hunch is that a group of substandard teachers who cannot attract students for tuition to earn easy money must have filed a complaint with the higher authority out of jealousy; but the unfortunate thing is that these teachers are incompetent and that is why students do not go to them."

Legislative initiatives were also stimulated by crises of various kinds. Box 5.2 refers to a fire in Gujarat State, which led to attention there and elsewhere about the lack of fire-safety provisions (e.g. *India Legal*, 2019). Other concerns related to suicides (e.g. *Hindustan Times*, 2017; Iqbal, 2018), which contributed to a bill presented to India's national parliament (Patel, 2016) aiming to set up a Coaching Centres Regulatory Board. The bill was not immediately approved, but was noteworthy for both its rationale and advocated regulations. The rationale (Patel, 2016, p. 6) included awareness of the pressures in coaching institutions, and proposed clauses for the legislation included:

- ensure the appointment of counsellor, psychiatrist and physiologist in every coaching centre for counselling of students; and
- suggest steps to be taken by every coaching centre for reducing psychological pressure on students.

However, the notion that every centre should appoint a counsellor, psychiatrist and physiologist was clearly not realistic. Similarly, managers of tutoring centres in Maharashtra arguably had a valid point when protesting against a planned regulation for separate toilets for boys and girls even if they only served 10 students in a

> **Box 5.2 Coaching centres in India – A case for regulation**
>
> The following text is from a newspaper article about regulations. It was written shortly after a serious fire in Surat, Gujarat, led to the deaths of 22 students in a coaching centre. It presents the case for regulation to prevent similar incidents.
>
> Economic theories suggest that when markets fail, governments need to be brought in. Market failure may occur because of the presence of externalities or asymmetry in information. Governments are also important because they act to coordinate moral norms. On all these counts, coaching institutions emerge as the proverbial villains. Hidden behind legislations meant for tiny shops (Shops and Establishment Act) as 'other' business, they run an empire of evening incarcerations that arrest creative freedom. The big ones draw an entire generation of young minds and systematically erode their imagination. They ignite psychological disorders in students, undermine mainstream education, impose huge opportunity costs to students, charge an exorbitant fee which is often untaxed, and yet remain unaccountable (several court cases on breach of promise of refund are underway). This paints a picture of coaching centres as market bullies. The social costs are exacerbated by the absolute disregard for the well-being of students, who are shoved into tiny rooms with little ventilation, let alone a fire exit. Society bears the burden — only for the sake of finding out who is marginally better than the other in cramming for some exam.
>
> The building in Surat had an illegally constructed terrace. It had a wooden staircase that got burnt, thus disabling any possibility of escape. It had no fire safety equipment, nor any compliance or inspection certificate. The response of the State government was to shut down all coaching institutions in Gujarat until fire inspections were completed. This was a typical knee-jerk reaction.
>
> The building which caught fire was located in a premise that was supposed to be a residential space, according to the approved plan of 2001. In 2007, a two-floor commercial complex was illegally built. It was legalised in 2013 under Gujarat's regularisation laws. The other floors where the fire broke out were constructed illegally later. With such patterns of violating the laws, these inspections will only serve a tick-mark purpose. But here is the point. Although government measures are more emotional than rational, they have achieved the purpose of drawing our attention to coaching centres. In the last six months, three fire incidents have involved coaching institutions in Gujarat.
>
> Source: Goyal (2019).

home (OpIndia, 2018). Such matters underlined the importance of regulations being reasonable, without which they will be ignored and called into disrepute.

At the same time, many schools feel threatened by the coaching centres. As children grow older and ascend the grades, they increasingly respect the tutors and coaching centres rather than their school teachers, and increasingly skip lessons in the schools in order to attend classes in the coaching centres (Bhorkar & Bray, 2018). Nevertheless, the schools are to some extent protected by the requirement for students to be registered in schools in order to sit the official examinations. Also, the examination boards require science students to have conducted some practical work which needs laboratories that are available in schools but not in most coaching centres.

Alongside the coaching centres is much informal tutoring. Bhorkar (2021, p. 21) remarked that regulations for these activities were even more deficient. Having remarked that most states still treat tutorial centres as commercial establishments, thereby allowing them to circumvent the regulatory procedures for setting up educational institutions, she added (p. 21) that "there are no regulations of any kind on the tutoring centres that are home-based, where tutors teach students at their or the students' homes".

5.4 Prominent features within the overall picture

Two specific features of the Indian scene also deserve note. One is geographic, namely India's famous "[shadow] educational city". The other concerns giant companies and the influence of the technology sector.

The so-called "educational city" is Kota, in Rajasthan. As recounted by Rao (2017), economic crisis hit the city in the 1980s and 1990s because strikes and shortage of raw materials beset the city's industrial units. Rejuvenation came through coaching centres able to attract students not only from the city and its environs but also from elsewhere in the state and beyond. Each year these coaching centres served 140,000 to 200,000 students, who also had needs for accommodation, food, transport and other necessities. Again, though, various negative dimensions were evident. On a procedural matter, the coaching institutes contributed to corruption insofar as they relied on "dummy" schools to register students so that those students could sit the public examinations even though no classes were ever taken in the schools. Even more salutary were suicides, specifically in Kota City (as well as elsewhere in India), arising from the pressures to which students were subjected. These events did lead to a form of self-regulation, but critics lamented that such measures were necessary.

On another note, a parallel with patterns in China has been evident in the way that large technology companies have entered the sector and exerted their influences. A prominent example in 2021 was the acquisition by Byju's, described as "the country's largest online edtech start-up", of Aakash Coaching. This company had a history of 33 years as a "brick-and-mortar" coaching enterprise, and was acquired for nearly US$1 billion (*The Hindu*, 2021). Byju's had been founded in 2011. It already claimed 90 million students on its e-learning platform, with 5.5 million annual paid subscribers and an annual renewal rate of 86% (Qureshi, 2021), and had previously acquired three other companies:

- in 2017, TutorVista and Edurite, from Pearson which is one of the largest publishing and online tutoring brands for school and college students in the US;
- in 2019, US-based Osmo, a blended-learning educational games platform for children aged 3-8 years; and
- in 2020, WhiteHat Jr, which teaches online coding to students through live lessons and interactive classes.

Following the acquisition of Aakash, Byju's indicated that it would launch new types of centres that were partially online and offline. The developments demonstrated the huge corporatisation at one end of the tutoring sector, together with the influence of technologies.

5.5 Summary

The Indian case again shows that efforts to ban private tutoring cannot succeed, and that instead an appropriate government role should be steering and regulating. Taking the country as a whole, a major constraint becomes evident in the decentralised system; but the corollary is that actors at the state and even lower levels can take action without waiting for the national authorities.

The Indian experience also demonstrates the need to secure some sort of consensus when moving to regulations. Efforts at regulation may stall because of protests from tutoring providers and even families. Further, even teachers may have vested interests when they are themselves providing tutoring and/or delegate parts of their roles to the supplementary sector (Ghosh & Bray, 2020; Gupta, 2022). As in Japan and China, a balance is needed between state intervention and market operation. The Chinese and Japanese governments have largely succeeded in finding balances, but the Indian authorities have been less successful. Resistance from the deep institutionalisation could be mediated through encouragement of self-regulation and through education of the consumers to improve transparency of market information; but that requires the authorities first to devise policies that are realistic and second to follow-through with enactment once those policies have been announced.

Of course, again as in Japan and China, balance is also needed in economic, social and educational dimensions. Companies are attracted by the potential profits from increased dependency of students on private tutoring, enhanced by technological advances. The national and sub-national governments understandably wish to support economic development and creation of employment, but that needs to be achieved within a framework that also respects social and educational dimensions. Moreover, a bottom line must surely be respected in terms of safety (for tutoring facilities and child protection); and at a higher level the authorities should consider the extent to which shadow education becomes a replacement for schooling with corrupting effects in terms of priorities. As such, the focus on tutoring in the revised National Education Policy (India, Ministry of Human Resource Development, 2020, p. 29) seems a significant step in an appropriate direction.

6 Egypt
Teachers as Tutors

6.1 Informal and school-organised tutoring

In Egypt, provision of supplementary tutoring by teachers has a long history. Chapter 2 mentioned Egypt's 1947 regulations, which prohibited teachers from offering private lessons either inside or outside schools without permission from their school authorities and the Ministry of Education (Egypt, 1947). Teachers who did receive permission were still prohibited from tutoring pupils for whom those teachers administered official examinations. The fact that the Ministry issued these regulations implies that the phenomenon was already significant and probably longstanding. The regulations were issued during an era when Egypt did not have an official policy about universal education, and state-provided schooling was relatively modest (Tadros, 2006, p. 238).

Marked change was brought in 1952 with the revolution led by Gamal Abdel Nasser, and his subsequent presidency lasting until 1970 with much socialist emphasis (Folmar, 2020). Schooling was massively expanded, and by 1959 government expenditures on education reached almost 48% of the total budget (Tadros, 2006, p. 239). The educational expansion also required employment of unqualified teachers and, in urban areas, double shifts (Hartmann, 2008, p. 21). Deteriorating quality was among the factors fuelling demand for shadow education.

Nasser was followed as president by Anwar Sadat (1970–1981), who moved away from Nasser's socialism. He faced an economic crisis and the need for structural adjustment to give market forces greater rein. The right to free education was not openly rescinded, but in practice was eroded. The further expansion of shadow education was part of this erosion. Teachers' salaries were reduced in real terms, pressing teachers to secure additional incomes from tutoring and/or other means.

DOI: 10.4324/9781003318453-9

Egypt's next president, Hosni Mubarak (1981–2011), sought to tackle at least some of the challenges. In 1983 his Minister of Education (quoted in Hartmann, 2008, p. 47) acknowledged that "The overspreading phenomenon of private lessons whether in schools or universities has become one of the major drawbacks in the education system." One measure to counter the phenomenon was a 1986 law requiring schools to offer supplementary tutoring, albeit fee-charging.

The possibility for schools to provide such tutoring had been introduced as early as 1952 (Hartmann, 2013, p. 62; Herrera, 2022, p. 47), and the 1986 law made it mandatory. The goal was to combat external tutoring and to alleviate part of its financial burden on families through lower prices. However, as observed by Sobhy Ramadan (2012, p. 95), the strategy "not only failed, but fuelled the ... tutoring dependence". The regulations stipulated that 85% of the income generated from in-school tutoring would go to the teachers and 15% to the administration at different levels. This created clear incentives to encourage such tutoring. Tadros (2006, pp. 241–244) provided evocative examples of ways in which families were forced to comply, and of disregard for regulations about maximum class size, conditions for fee exemption and designated fee levels.

During the 1990s, numerical data became available through national surveys. A 1991/92 survey cited by Hua (1996, p. 12) found that 54% of sampled Grade 5 students and 74% of sampled Grade 8 students were receiving some form of supplementary tutoring. A related survey, though with a smaller sample (Fergany, 1994, p. 79), reported that private tutoring consumed 20% of total household expenditures per child in urban primary schools and 15% in rural primary schools. A The World Bank report (2002, p. 26) indicated that at least 8.8% of total Gross Domestic Product (GDP) was devoted to education, of which 60% was publicly managed and as much as 40% was privately managed. These figures far exceeded averages for members of the Organisation for Economic Co-operation and Development (OECD); and within these expenditure estimates, shadow education was estimated to represent 1.6% of GDP. The World Bank report added that although a Ministerial Decree (Egypt, 1998) had banned teachers in both public and private schools from providing tutoring outside their school-managed arrangements, "the practice of tutoring remains unabated".

The end of the Mubarak era in 2011 brought regime change, but some consistency in government attitudes towards private tutoring. A Prime Ministerial Decree (Egypt, 2013) stipulated that the Minister of Education and the Governors (i.e. the top administrators of each of the 27 sub-national governorates) had the right to send teachers who provided private tutoring for "administrative investigation". This did lead to action from one Governor, noted below, but that action was short-lived.

The generalised and persistent penetration of private tutoring was also evident in the subsequent years of the regime led by Abdel Fattah el-Sisi, who led a 2013 coup d'état and took over the presidency in 2014. A new constitution, approved in 2014, committed the government to expenditure on education equivalent to 4% of the Gross Domestic Product, but this could not be achieved (Springborg, 2021, p. 88). The authorities became more sympathetic to private schooling and even to charging fees in public schools, even if not to private tutoring.

On the topic of officially-sanctioned school-organised tutoring, in 2016 the fees were increased to allow for inflation and were also adjusted with variations by urban/rural location and grade (Sieverding et al. 2019, p. 568). For example urban fees for group tutoring in Grades 7 and 8 were set at 35 Egyptian pounds and for Grade 9 at 40 pounds. The revenue distributions were adjusted to 90% for the teachers, 5% for the schools and 5% for the teachers' union. Although schools had been required since 1986 to offer supplementary classes, the Ministry reiterated that enrolment in these classes was voluntary. Nevertheless, teachers and their schools continued to view it as a valued source of revenue, and continued to exert pressure on their students.

Alongside the tutoring provided in schools was much provision in the homes of students and/or teachers and in various public locations such as libraries, mosques and churches. Many students who could afford it preferred out-of-school tutoring, even if that tutoring was delivered by the same teachers (Box 6.1). This was because the teachers commonly behaved in a more client-oriented way when outside the schools. Home tutoring provided lessons on a one-to-one basis or in groups commonly comprising 4–10 students. Such tutoring was relatively costly, with prices varying according to the educational level and the importance of the subject. Student-teacher relationships were often close, with students receiving much more individual attention than during regular class hours at school. Most such lessons were provided in the afternoons and evenings, usually once or twice a week, for one or two hours.

During the 2010s, several sources provided valuable data. The 2012 Egypt Labor Market Panel Survey provided statistics by grade (Assaad & Krafft, 2015, p. 23). Even in Grade 1, 33% of surveyed students were receiving private lessons, and a further 9% were in fee-paying help groups. For Grade 6, these numbers were 61% and 12%. Further data were provided by the 2014 Survey of Young People in Egypt (Sieverding et al., 2019, p. 572). Among surveyed Grade 12 students, 72% were receiving private one-to-one tutoring and 18% private group tutoring. Related data from parents whose children were receiving tutoring indicated that for 50.3% of cases the tutors were the children's existing teachers (Ille & Peacey, 2019, p. 107). Then the 2018 iteration of the Egypt Labor Market Panel Survey showed increased receipt of shadow education compared with 2012 in all income quintiles except the poorest (Moreno Olmedilla, 2022, p. 152).

Box 6.1 Peer pressure, social competition and prestige

Parts of Hartmann's research (2013, p. 66) focused on why parents felt the need to invest in shadow education, including that provided by the students' own teachers. She observed that it had become an integral feature of the Egyptian education system. "Students fear missing something if they do not take part in the ubiquitous practice", she said. Analysing the reasons, Hartmann then cited the explanation of an interviewee:

> Even some of the best students take private lessons, because their parents think that they will benefit more if they see their teacher at home. Often they ask a particular teacher for lessons, because the student likes this teacher. It also has to do with envy or jealousy between the students. If one student asks a teacher to come to his home, the others want to do the same. Even if they don't really need the private lessons, if their friends do it, they want it, too. 'So Mr. Ehab teaches you at home? I will ask my father to get Mr. Ehab'. It is like saying: 'You are not richer than me, I can afford this teacher, too'.

In this upper-class family, Hartmann explained, private tutoring fulfilled social as well as educational functions. Similar factors to some extent operated in other socio-economic strata.

6.2 Tutorial centres as providers

Although many teachers organise their own out-of-school tutoring, others operate through tutorial centres. In Cairo, the first tutorial centres were established in the late 1970s and early 1980s (Hartmann, 2008, p. 72). At that time the centres mainly catered for middle-class families, but mushrooming of enterprises during the mid-1990s expanded the reach to all socio-economic groups albeit with concentration in urban centres (Sobhy Ramadan, 2012, p. 96). Some tutors in these centres were independent entrepreneurs. Most striking among them were the "famous tutors" with strong market appeal. Some taught only small groups, which permitted them to charge individuals, particularly high prices, but others secured much greater total incomes with lower prices and huge classes. Hartmann (2008, p. 62) referred to a tutorial centre in Cairo with up to 1,200 students in a class. This was at the extreme, but classes of 300 to 500 students were relatively common (see also Herrera, 2022, p. 103).

The total size of the sector, even in the contemporary era, has been difficult to estimate. Thus, Moreno Olmedilla (2022, p. 153) remarked that government data was virtually non-existent and that "it is truly a shadow industry, mostly informal, underground and fiscally opaque". Nevertheless, informal evidence provides descriptors. Small centres serve perhaps 10–15 students at a time and operate in ordinary apartment buildings, but larger enterprises may have multiple branches. The centres particularly focus on the end of secondary schooling *thanawiyya 'amma* examinations. As noted by Abdel-Moneim (2021, p. 6), sometimes the venues utilised by famous tutors are divided so that some students directly see the tutors but others occupy separate rooms with video screens.

Many of these centres have no legal basis, but some are operated by non-governmental organisations (NGOs) regulated by Law 32 of 1964 which requires registration with the Ministry of Social Affairs (MOSA) (Hartmann, 2008, p. 48). The MOSA prohibits political activism, and has far-reaching powers to control its workings. Centres that do not register with the MOSA risk being closed, and even when they do register they may remain vulnerable to Ministry of Education strictures. As such, circumstances are fluid. Moreno Olmedilla (2022, p. 156) remarked on the ineffectiveness of regulations over the decades, adding that private tutoring "keeps getting stronger, under the nose of the government, and in plain sight even though it walks the fine line between legality and illegality".

Following the promulgation of the Prime Ministerial decree noted above (Egypt, 2013), one striking incident occurred in the Al-Sharkeyya governorate (El Watan, 2015; Abdel-Moneim, 2021, p. 3). Empowered by the decree, the Governor decided to take action by closing the (illegal) tutorial centres in his governorate and fining their owners 50,000 Egyptian pounds (US$6,400). To provide an alternative, he accompanied his action with enhanced support for in-school tutoring. However, demonstrations not only by the owners of the tutorial centres but also by parents and students escalated into a crisis that led the Governor to resign within a month of launching the initiative.

The Al-Sharkeyya events demonstrated the strength of tutoring consumers as well as tutoring providers. Similar remarks apply to the 2018 proposal by the Deputy Minister of Education to criminalise unauthorised tutorial centres (Al-Youm, 2018). The original proposal again envisaged a fine of up to 50,000 Egyptian pounds for anyone providing tutoring in a centre or a public location, and the penalty was then increased to imprisonment for not less than one year and not more than three years in the case of repeating the crime. However, the proposal was not approved by Parliament (*Egypt Independent*, 2021). Further, the taxation authorities dissented from the implication that because tutorial centres were illegal, the operators could not pay tax.

6.3 Trying a different approach

A consistent theme in the Egyptian research on private tutoring has been the extent to which "supplementary" has ceased to be an appropriate word, at least in the senior grades of secondary schooling, because in those grades tutoring has to a large extent displaced schooling. To illustrate, the majority of Abdel-Moneim's (2021) interviewees skipped the last year of schooling in order to join tutoring classes. They did visit the schools to complete forms required to sit the final examination, but other visits were mainly to pay fees, meet friends and get textbooks. Moreover, even if they had attended school they would likely have found that the teachers were not motivated to teach empty classrooms. Abdel-Moneim reported (p. 5) that in a few cases some students found teachers willing to teach, but one interviewee did not even know the names of her school teachers. Another only went to school for the first two weeks to avoid dismissal, but found that there were no classes to attend. When this student was dismissed from school because of non-attendance, she and her friends paid a nominal financial penalty for re-enrolment (which was required for sitting the examination), and continued their absence.

Recognising the challenge to schooling, in 2018 the government launched an ambitious reform with a five-year budget of US$2,000 million of which US$500 million was provided through a World Bank loan. A major goal, in the words of the Minister of Education (quoted by Saavedra 2019), was "to bring learning back to the classroom". As explained by Moreno Olmedilla (2022, p. 156), the Ministry of Education assumed that more regulation would not make a difference and that the goal should rather be "to understand how to create an environment which would fundamentally change the need, or perception of need, for private lessons, and lead to different practices and behaviors". That included examination reform and, most dramatically, the replacement of the external *thanawiyya 'amma* examination by school-based assessments. Further, even the World Bank (2018, p. iv) assigned an overall high-risk rating to the project, describing macroeconomics as a "substantial" risk and placing politics and governance in the category of "high" risk (Bray, 2021b, p. 71).

Adding substance to this remark, Moreno Olmedilla praised the ambition of the project but also noted that some fundamentals were adjusted even in 2019 and were further threatened by administrative measures necessitated in 2020 by the outbreak of COVID-19 (see also El Baradei, 2022). Thus, in particular, the proposal to base final assessment on the Grade Point Averages (GPAs) of tests in the previous three years had been abandoned by 2021. Moreno Olmedilla did not expect the remaining aspects of the reform to remove tutoring, but still felt that it might harness the sector through changed client demand. He particularly had in mind the component of computer-based open-book tests, and emphasised (p. 156) that:

> If the education reform succeeds in changing the focus of the private tutoring culture, both on the supply and the demand sides, from rote learning to relevant skills and competences, Egypt would have used the very strength of such a culture to transition to a modern education system that delivers genuine learning for all students.

That, however, was a big "if". Vested interests had long triumphed in Egypt, and even the parents were not united in opposition to shadow education. This had been demonstrated in the 2015 experience in Al-Sharkeyya governorate. More broadly, as noted by Abdel-Moneim (2021, p. 11), parental protest against closure of tutorial centres could be seen as irrational in the sense that these institutions drained their resources, but could also be seen as parental and student defence of their right to education.

Thus, in Egypt private tutoring has become deeply engrained in the cultures of both families and teachers. In earlier decades, it was particularly linked to low teachers' salaries, and to some extent that link remains. However, a 2012 hike in salaries was unable to achieve a significant dent in teacher-provided tutoring (Ille & Peacey, 2019, p. 107), and further signals are evident elsewhere. Many Egyptian teachers have migrated to the prosperous countries of the Arabian Gulf, where they receive considerably higher salaries but still provide private tutoring. They do so in part because, as presented by interviewees to Ridge et al. (2017, p. 47) "it is part of their identity".

6.4 Summary

Egypt has a long history of private tutoring, especially that provided by teachers and, since the latter decades of the 20th century, by tutorial centres (many of which themselves employed teachers on a part-time basis). Private tutoring has firmly entered the culture and has shown constant resistance to regulation. As a result, many of the regulations that do exist are only on paper; and an irony of the fact that most tutorial centres are actually illegal is that they operate even more in the shadows than would be the case if some sort of commercial and perhaps also educational regulations made them more legitimate and accountable.

Among the measures taken by successive governments has been first encouragement and then requirement for schools to offer school-managed tutoring for government-determined prices. Yet ironically this measure has provided incentives for teachers and administrators to expand that form of supplementary tutoring while also failing to quench the various forms of external tutoring. The 2018 reform was a bold vision through an alternative tack, but within one year had undergone some adjustments and then required further change in the face of COVID-19. In the competition between schooling and shadow education, it remains uncertain which side will win.

7 Denmark
Students as Tutors

7.1 Context and emergence of shadow education

Compared with the other four countries in this part of the book, Denmark is a small country with a population of only approximately 5.8 million. In common with its Scandinavian neighbours, it is renowned for excellence in the public school system.

For many decades, shadow education in this context was barely noticeable. Bray's (2011) survey of patterns in the European Union remarked (p. 25) that Northern Europe, in contrast to Eastern, Southern and Western Europe, had to date been least affected by the rise of private tutoring:

> Scandinavian countries seem to maintain stronger traditions of schools adequately meeting their students' needs. Certainly students in Scandinavia receive extra lessons, both to help slow learners keep up with their peers and to stretch the learning of high achievers; but much of this work is provided within the framework of public schooling rather than through a parallel system.

Yet the following decade brought significant shifts, with patterns in the individual Scandinavian countries to some extent influencing each other (Christensen & Zhang, 2021).

Elaborating with specific reference to Denmark, strong ideals during the second half of the 20th century stressed opportunities for all children regardless of their social or economic backgrounds. Education was viewed as much more than academic achievement and performance, and parents were content to rely on the state for educational direction and support. However, the turn of the century brought some shifts. A 2000 report by the Danish Center for Social Science Research cited by Mikkelsen and Gravesen (2021, p. 556) highlighted

DOI: 10.4324/9781003318453-10

ambivalence. Focusing on competition between children, the report noted divided parental opinions: "Thus, there is a considerable resistance against competition in a general sense (e.g. between children in school), alongside an acceptance of elements of competition in well-defined areas (e.g. in sports and games)". The fact that most parents resisted competition in school reflected the history of democracy and equality, and underpinned stress on whole-person development rather than academic achievement and performance.

This perspective evolved further during the following years. Globalisation was a broad force for change, and more specific was Denmark's mediocre performance – especially in comparison with Finland – in the surveys of the Programme for International Student Assessment (PISA) managed by the Organisation for Economic Co-operation and Development (OECD). Mikkelsen and Gravesen (2021) observed that education, high performance and competencies were now considered necessary for economic wealth and continuance of the welfare state. For children and parents, they added (p. 553):

> this has led to more pressure to do well in school to live up to the expectations of society. In conjunction with school reforms, such new views on education, academic skills, and performance lead parents to reflect on the role of education in new ways, and accordingly, perhaps be less reluctant to buy private supplementary tutoring.

A specific trigger for expansion of shadow education was a 2013 teachers' strike and then lockout which closed the schools and caused much parental anxiety (Høgedahl & Ibsen, 2017). The founder of MentorDanmark, the company that is now the dominant player in private tutoring, stressed in a 2019 interview with the author that he was neither seeking to undermine the strike/lockout nor to exploit it as a business opportunity (Zhang, 2021b, p. 616). However, the environment was certainly conducive to his idea of providing educational support through the private sector.

The history of MentorDanmark has also been evocatively told by its founder and Chief Executive Officer (CEO) in a journal article (Kany, 2021). This history is one of small beginnings leading to expansion through hard work and careful strategising to reach the stage at which the company has about 80% of the market. Nevertheless, alongside this company are many smaller operations, some of them established by former employees of MentorDanmark. Christensen et al. (2021, p. 526) identified 62 such companies, noting that most, like MentorDanmark, had been established since 2012.

7.2 Business models

The survey of Danish enterprises by Christensen et al. (2021) included remarks on business models (p. 528). First, the authors noted, individual tutoring was by far the most common mode of delivery. Large classes seemed to be completely absent, and even small classes were very rare. Tutoring in groups of up to three students was relatively common, but was presented by the companies as a way to reduce prices rather than as a tutoring format in its own right.

Concerning the locations, home tutoring was the dominant model. None of the ten companies that Christensen et al. (2021) examined in detail provided tutoring on their own premises, and only two companies provided online tutoring as their core service. One of these two companies provided instructional videos supplemented by online personal tutoring, while the other offered personalised and customised online tutoring. All the other companies offered offline, face-to-face, individualised tutoring. One company had an online platform, but it functioned as a kind of "dating agency" to match students and tutors for personal interaction that was then conducted offline.

Further fieldwork by the author and colleagues confirmed and elaborated on the above picture. As in other countries, the shape of shadow education is much influenced by the shape of schooling. Schools, and teachers within schools, have much autonomy to devise their own curricula. This has meant that providers of tutoring cannot easily operate large classes serving students from multiple schools with standardised curricula and that instead, providers must offer much individualised support. Danish culture also has a clear division between schooling, leisure-time education and family education. Tutoring is considered by parents as a private matter that should be provided in the private rather than public space. Reflecting these perspectives, one-to-one home tutoring was reported to be the dominant form.

Also significant – and in sharp contrast to dominant patterns in India and Egypt, for example – was that school teachers were rarely involved. Only one of the 10 companies reviewed by Christensen et al. (2021, p. 530) – the one offering videos in conjunction with online personalised tutoring – employed professional teachers as tutors. While most company founders and Chief Executive Officers (CEOs) had some background in teaching, almost all their tutors were university and secondary-school students. One company had employed preservice teachers but had ceased operation. Most of the school students employed as tutors were in upper secondary, but at least one company employed lower secondary students.

MentorDanmark was the largest company in the group analysed by Christensen et al. (2021) – and became even larger after buying out the company offering videos in conjunction with online personalised tutoring. Kany (2021) explained that focus on one-to-one tutoring in the homes of tutees was deemed a good model in part because it avoided investment in classrooms or other premises for the conduct of tutoring. The inspiration for this model had been taken from MyAcademy, a Swedish counterpart that had been operating in Denmark but withdrew in the face of competition. MentorDanmark's two basic formats of tutoring were one-to-one on a weekly basis for nine months, and intensive one-to-one help for forthcoming examinations. The services were offered for both primary and secondary school students.

Continuing his story, Kany (2021, p. 632) recalled that when the 2013 conflict between the government and teachers was resolved, it also brought a school-system reform:

> One of the major changes was the establishment of mandatory homework cafés where children now were expected to do homework and preparations, something that had not been mandatory before, where children usually did homework at home; consequently, the media now called MentorDanmark clappedout/ doomed, and predicted that there would not be a demand for our tutoring or courses.

The reality, however, was completely different. Kany continued (pp. 632–633):

> In our first year, we experienced a tripling of the demand, and the year after that another doubling. Our concept was well-received nationwide, and the recommendations traveled through word of mouth from families that used our services.

The establishment of mandatory homework cafés, Kany argued, sent a clear signal to the parents about the need for extra help.

> We often heard stories of cafés being staffed by only one teacher or pedagogue, and this single person being assigned to help two to three entire classes, around 80 students simultaneously. This was an error in priorities from a rather large reform. Naturally, this, in turn, led to the parents seeking alternatives and calling MentorDanmark.

Christensen et al. (2021) echoed the view that the reform had legitimised homework support as a need (or right) for all students but fell short of the expectations that it had itself created. Thus, "there are indications that the provision of public homework cafés served to amplify, rather than dampen trends toward increased use of private tutoring" (p. 540). This episode exemplifies unanticipated consequences of government reform as noted in Chapter 3 on Japan and evident elsewhere (see e.g. Altinyelken, 2013).

Elaborating on the decision to employ students as tutors, Kany (2021, p. 633) explained that the idea was a "young-to-younger" concept:

> We had to be much more than just tutoring. An educator at MentorDanmark should also function as a role model that a student could look up to. Therefore, the term "mentor" was best suited.

Kany added that from a more pedagogical viewpoint, the term mentor had fewer negative connotations, which meant that the parents had fewer issues convincing their children to participate. "If we had called them teachers, educators, tutors, or something similar, our conviction was that the students would believe something was wrong with them as they had to have extra aid, which was to be avoided if possible" (p. 633).

Expanding demand required a greater supply of tutors, so the company in due course added secondary students to the team alongside university students. None of these tutors could be called professionals, though the company did run orientation workshops with tips on ways to proceed. The company stressed the importance of matching the tutees' personalities and learning styles with those of the tutors, highlighting motivation and study skills more than academic content. By 2019, the company had approximately 2,300 tutors on its list. About 65% of the clients were in primary schools, and the remainder were in secondary schools. The emphasis was strongly on remedial support for students who were struggling to keep up rather than on enrichment to enhance the skills of the top performers.

Elaborating on the significance of vocabulary, evident not only in the decision to call its tutors "mentors" but also in the decision to call the clients "families", contrasts were evident in the names of competing companies. Thus, one competing (but much smaller) company commenced by calling itself GoodGrade but found that this had been an unwise decision in the Danish egalitarian culture, and in 2019 changed its name to GoodTutor. Another enterprise called FixMyAssignment offered help with assessments for college admission but closed following critique about supporting plagiarism and providing giving unfair advantages to families that could pay (Christensen et al., 2021, p. 521).

Finally, the impact of COVID-19 needs attention. Kany remarked (2021, p. 638) that like so many other businesses MentorDanmark received a massive blow when the crisis hit in early 2020:

> Suddenly, everything we had achieved seemed to be in danger. Almost overnight, demand for our services fell by 80%–90%. Instead, we scrambled to retain the customers we already had. Parents had never shown interest in online tutoring and almost all our services were therefore conducted on an offline/physical basis. Furthermore, a vast number of examinations were canceled, which reduced the need for private tutoring.

Nevertheless, he added:

> we persuaded the majority of parents to continue tutoring on an online basis. At the same time, we tried to help schools and students as best as we could. A total of 300 of our mentors volunteered for an online tutoring service, which we offered for free to all students in the country.

In December 2020, Denmark went into a second lockdown and Kany again feared a catastrophic decline in demand. This time, however, parents seemed more prepared and the company was less affected. Looking ahead, Kany observed that both tutors and students had become much more adept at online approaches to teaching and learning. However, the COVID-19 crisis also created profound "online fatigue". As a result, Kany felt (2021, p. 638): "More than ever, students and parents demand the intimacy of face-to-face tutoring." Thus, even if online tutoring was set to become more significant, the company's focus on offline, face-to-face tutoring had stood the test of the COVID-19 crisis. In these domains, cultural factors were evident. Whereas Chinese companies seized the COVID-19 crisis as an opportunity to expand online tutoring, MentorDanmark persisted through the crisis and then shifted to provide special-needs education and strengthen partnerships with schools for homework support.

7.3 Patterns of (non-)regulation

Christensen et al. (2021, p. 524) observed that in Denmark private supplementary tutoring "still leads a shadowy existence". They added that in contrast to Sweden, for example (Hallsén, 2021), private tutoring "remains ignored in education policy and largely unmonitored by public authorities – both in terms of regulation and data collection". In general, Danish society is highly regulated; but because the shadow education sector is in its infancy, legislation has not yet caught up with its emergence. Enterprises are regulated as companies in the commercial sector, but no specific guidelines or requirements for the tutoring sector have yet been set by the government. Much administration of education is conducted at the municipal level. Copenhagen Municipality is by far the largest in population and in this and other respects the most significant. A key legislator in Copenhagen Municipality interviewed by the author in 2019 showed awareness of developments in the shadow education sector, but was more concerned about private schools than tutoring companies.

The sorts of regulations that might usefully be explored concern not only premises, contracts, accounting and other domains considered in this book but also arrangements concerning university and secondary school students. Christensen et al. (2021, p. 530) state that companies generally demand top grades in the subjects that tutor applicants want to teach, and, as mentioned, MentorDanmark runs orientation workshops with tips on how to proceed. However, this cannot be taken as professional training.

Further, the fact that many (perhaps most) of the secondary school students are under the age of 18 raises legal questions about responsibilities. Again to cite Christensen et al. (2021, p. 530), at least some companies require applicants to have clean criminal records; but the fact that most tutoring takes place in private homes raised potential issues about sexual abuse and related problems. The authorities might need to consider the structures that companies have in place to address these matters. Chapter 2 noted that the government of Western Australia (2018) allows tutors to work in public schools on certain conditions including that each tutor and has had a National Criminal Record History Check (NCRHC) and a Working with Children Check (WWCC). Tutors must have public liability insurance, and have written agreements with the students' parents or guardians. Counterpart regulations might be imposed on tutorial companies in Denmark, i.e. requiring such checks and securing such public liability insurance.

Alongside the companies, of course, are likely many students and others who provide tutoring independently rather than through companies. Tutors in these categories are even more difficult to regulate. Their arrangements may not even have written contracts, and income is not declared for taxation. In such circumstances perhaps the best route lies in educating the consumer, i.e. calling to parental attention some of the risks and explaining what safeguards might exist, alongside mechanisms to tackle issues if and when they arise. The mechanisms might include liaison with schools and an approach to consumer councils. These processes of educating consumers would also help families to hold the companies accountable. Yet although the process of educating the consumers would bring the topic out of the shadows, authorities may be reluctant to do so because they have other priorities.

7.4 Summary

Kany (2021, p. 631) observed that after emergence much later than most other parts of the world, the market for tutoring in Denmark remained small but had become significant. He added that "private tutoring is increasingly viewed as a viable business and not just as a source of pocket money or supplementary income". Yet he also highlighted some of the challenges and resistance that he met as an entrepreneur "in this new and, to some, controversial market". Danish attitudes towards family self-help through private expenditures have evolved and will evolve further, yet remain complex.

This theme was elaborated upon by Christensen et al. (2021). Recognising that the scale of tutoring is currently very limited, they observed the major reason that "its moral viability and legitimacy remains very much in question" (p. 532). Christensen et al. did not view a ban on private tutoring as being on the agenda but added that:

> it remains highly contested whether private tutoring is morally feasible – that is, whether a market in private tutoring can be made consistent with commonly accepted social definitions of education, parenting, and childhood and with more general social values of fairness, equality, and social cohesion.

Yet the very fact that Danes, including parents who invest in tutoring, keep questioning its moral viability and legitimacy set some moral boundaries in the tutoring marketplace. Beliefs shaped by the egalitarian ideology and the philosophy of natural education have made tutoring providers adapt to such values with claimed foci on learning motivation, confidence and commitment to reduce learning gaps (Zhang, 2021b). By doing so, they have gradually gained legitimacy.

As such, Danish culture plays a role in regulating tutoring – perhaps more effectively than laws and regulations. In China, the fierce government regulations receive limited public support, in part because they conflict with perceptions of the parental responsibility to support their children to excel in the intensely competitive and hierarchical society. In Denmark, by contrast, cultural perceptions safeguard the educational orientations of tutoring via the press, peer pressures and the public guilt of tutoring providers and consumers, leading to strong social regulation in the absence of significant government regulation.

Within this picture, market activity in Denmark has been noteworthy since the early 2010s, and can only be expected to expand. In these circumstances, the authorities might be well advised to look at the sector more closely. This chapter has noted most tutoring is face-to-face in person rather than online, and that most tutors are university and school students who work with the tutees in their own homes. Also distinctive is the focus on well-being and the whole child rather than just scores in tests and examinations. These emphases differ from those in other countries and arguably require different forms of government oversight.

Part III
Conclusions

8 Learning from Comparing

8.1 Aspirations, mandates and goals

A starting point for this book was the United Nations' Sustainable Development Goals, and specifically the fourth goal (SDG4) which, to recall, is to "Ensure inclusive and equitable quality education and promote lifelong learning opportunities for all" by 2030 (UNESCO, 2017a). At the outset, the book observed that if left to market forces, private supplementary tutoring is likely to be *ex*clusive and *in*equitable and thus to pull in the opposite direction to SDG4. In this context, regulations are needed to harness the sector and to help achieve wider goals of social protection.

Yet at the national level, a necessary question is how governments see their roles. Ministries of Education, in particular, may feel that their remit is mainly or exclusively about schooling, and that oversight of shadow education is therefore beyond their domain of responsibility. This is part of the reason for *laissez faire* approaches in many countries. This book argues that at least assessment and monitoring of the scale, nature and impact of shadow education must be undertaken by governments. First, shadow education has become a major component of the overall landscape in most countries, and second shadow education has a backwash on schooling. Third, international experience shows that by the time governments recognise the importance of regulating tutoring, they have usually missed the timing for effective shaping and steering of the sector.

An example of timing that was arguably belated has been provided in the chapter on China. When the government did decide to regulate tutoring, the industry was already large and entrenched. The large companies had their own vested interests and ways of doing things, and the small companies had ways to avoid visibility. Nevertheless, the national, provincial and local authorities did tackle issues with determination, resulting in significant achievements. The Indian case is an even more instructive example where tutoring is so entrenched in the culture that regulations encounter strong resistance. The Egyptian authorities did introduce regulations at an early date but were unable to follow up effectively and again found that shadow education became a deep component of the culture.

Another challenge in all countries is the speed of change in the tutoring sector. In South Africa, data collected through a carefully-administered national sample under the umbrella of the Southern and Eastern Africa Consortium for Measuring Educational Quality (SACMEQ) indicated an increase in private-tutoring enrolment rates of Grade 6 students from 4.0% in 2007 to 29.1% in 2013 (Bray, 2021b, p. 17). Further review showed regional disparities, with 2013 enrolment rates ranging from 10.5% in Limpopo to 61.5% in Free State. Beyond these statistics, little information is available to explain the sudden shift but to some extent it reflected local, national and international entrepreneurs taking advantage of market opportunities. As in other countries, the government's lack of attention to the sector permitted such dramatic growth in a largely unregulated environment.

Across the planet, moreover, the 2010s were marked by technological developments on an unprecedented scale. Although consequential shifts were evident in mainstream schooling, conservatism in the sector restricted the pace of change. The tutoring sector by contrast was relatively unconstrained by traditions and bureaucracies, and seized opportunities to provide online and mixed-mode teaching with unprecedented speed. The pace was accelerated in 2020 by the COVID-19 pandemic when face-to-face tutoring was largely prohibited and companies therefore had to innovate in order to survive.

Online tutoring, however, is even more difficult to regulate than face-to-face tutoring. To date, China is the only country to have devised comprehensive regulations for online tutoring – yet again needing constant updating, for example to accommodate dual-tutor programs by AI tutors. Such experience is instructive for countries, e.g. in Central Africa, where the scale of tutoring is still limited and online tutoring scarce. Once again, policy makers would be wise to regulate and steer tutoring in the early stage when tutoring is within the reach and capacity of the government. For countries like India, where online tutoring is expanding at great speed but largely left to the market, government commitment is needed to regulate the sector to protect consumers and providers, and to limit its backwash on public schooling.

In all these domains, partnerships are needed. Tutorial centres operating as businesses should to some extent be regulated in partnership with the Ministry of Commerce or equivalent; and regulation of online tutoring requires support from Cyberspace Administration or equivalent. The most obvious needs for regulation concern the safety of buildings, contractual arrangements, accounting, and taxation. Safety issues may include attention to fire regulations in conjunction with the Ministry of Housing or equivalent. Issues related to crimes such as child abuse and violence call for involvement of the police force. Shadow education is in nature a hybrid of commercial, social and educational undertakings. Regulating shadow education is only possible from joint actions of all relevant departments for both policy making and policy enforcement.

8.2 From vision to enactment

Even when governments do wish to regulate shadow education, they may not have enough staff with the right skills, or sufficient financial and technical resources. Inspections and follow-up are demanding, and require coordination not only between national and provincial (or equivalent) governments but also local authorities and even schools. All the above also involves financial costs. Technologies, if used well as in Shanghai, can help reduce the input of human and financial resources, but their use can raise further questions about privacy.

At the same time, much depends on cultural issues. Acceptance of the need for regulation has perhaps increased in recent years because of evident abuses, some of which have received much media attention. In turn these relate to the scale of shadow education, which expanded with the arrival of the COVID-19 pandemic. A growing number of teachers in countries as different as the USA and Kenya have been sought by families for support in face of school closures or in dissatisfaction with disrupted schooling. These practices risked legitimising teachers' involvement in tutoring and driving more teachers to become tutors.

As in the domains of schooling and other spheres, a gap commonly exists between formulation and realisation of policies. Tutoring is less structured and more diverse than schooling, and detailed analysis of the types and providers of tutoring may be necessary. Policy interventions may be more effective in the hardware of premises than in the software of personnel and curricula, and government interventions may be mediated or even subverted by market dynamics.

These circumstances stress the importance of a balance between standardisation and diversity. As mentioned above, a starting point lies in differentiated requirements for different categories of tutoring providers. Experience in Japan has demonstrated that self-employed tutors and high-quality small enterprises may be valuable components of the education ecosystem able to cater for individual needs, and that elimination of these providers raises concerns about market concentration and monopoly.

Protection of the diversity and flexibility of tutoring lies in balances and partnerships between states, markets, families and civil societies. Voices of families and tutoring providers need to be heard in the policy text and process. Many families feel that tutoring, just as much as schooling, is a human right. Thus total bans on tutoring are not realistic. This was indeed demonstrated in the Republic of Korea, where the government in 1980 tried to ban private tutoring but found the position untenable to the point at which in 2000 the courts declared the ban unconstitutional (Bray, 2009, p. 52). As shown in the Japan chapter, official research on consumers of shadow education may widen the governments' perspectives and deepen understanding of how tutoring is perceived by families. Problematic dimensions do not come from all tutoring providers, nor from all tutoring practices. It is important to distinguish the right from the wrong. After all, when policy fails to work well, the fault may lie in the policy itself rather than in the tutoring providers. An alternative to the displacement of small centres by large companies might be the management of appropriate venues by non-education enterprises willing to take the administrative burden from small tutorial operations. Underutilised public facilities and social institutions may also be utilised for such purposes, and attention to broader social issues can help steer tutors towards lifelong education that broadens and changes the nature of the sector.

Further, the challenges in policy enactment for the shadow education sector commonly arise from mistrust on the sides of both government and tutoring providers. The Japanese and Chinese experiences show that the authorities can turn negativities into opportunities through active communication and support. Understanding challenges faced by tutoring providers in compliance, provision of timely support, and improvement of government services could help tutoring providers interpret the policy and comply. Partnerships with professional associations can enhance dialogue and mutual understanding and help find the common ground.

In these and other respects, measures leading to the professionalisation of tutoring are a key solution to in-service teachers' engagement in tutoring. In Japan and elsewhere, the roles of serving teachers in provision of supplementary tutoring have decreased to the point of almost total disappearance as tutoring enterprises have developed towards specialisation and professionalisation. Teachers' incentives to tutor have decreased as teacher welfare has improved, and fierce sanctions have been enforced on teacher involvement in tutoring. Yet elsewhere, fierce policies have been ignored because governments have neither the moral power nor the administrative machinery to enforce them.

8.3 Four takeaway messages

This section highlights four core messages, described as "takeaways". The first message is that shadow education will not simply go away, and should receive proper attention from policy-makers. The second message highlights the multiplicity of reference points for this policy attention. Allied, the third message stresses the need for policies on schooling and shadow education to be considered together; and the final one considers possibilities for partnerships.

Takeaway 1: Shadow education is here to stay

Historical analysis shows that in some countries shadow education has been a significant phenomenon at least from the early and mid-20th century. Patterns in Mauritius come to mind, as identified by Foondun (2002, p. 488) who quoted a 1901 statement by the head of what was then the only state secondary school for boys about negative dimensions of tutoring that he "felt helpless" to prevent. In Ceylon (Sri Lanka), a 1943 report strongly criticised the coaching institutions that helped students to cram for examinations (Kannangara, 1943, paras.116, 140, 309). In Egypt, as mentioned in Chapter 6, national regulations to control private tutoring were issued in 1947; and in the Republic of Korea, efforts at the top level of government to reduce private supplementary tutoring commenced in 1955 (Bray, 2009, p. 48).

Alongside these countries, as mentioned in Chapters 3 and 5, are long histories of shadow education in Japan and India. Yet in all these countries shadow education has actually expanded and intensified; and these countries have been joined by counterparts across the globe – including even Denmark (Chapter 7) and other Nordic countries (Christensen & Zhang, 2021). Government measures are needed to steer and regulate the sector, but it will never be eliminated. As observed above, experiences around the world have shown that governments, families and tutoring providers have to pay a huge price when the state intervention comes late. Regulating shadow education as early as possible could steer and shape it to contribute to the sustainable development of education ecosystems and minimise the damage of its negative impacts.

Persistence and commitment are also crucial. Compared to the Republic of Korea and China, the regulations were not effectively enforced in India, for example. This could be explained by the level of decentralisation in India, but also showed a lack of sustained effort from the national and state governments.

Takeaway 2: Policies for shadow education should encompass multiple reference points

Jurisdictions lagging in regulation of private tutoring can compare themselves with those ahead and consider what would (not) fit their local contexts. Tutoring policies and accompanying regulations around the world encompass three dimensions: commercial, educational and social. Classifying the many international policies on tutoring analysed in this report, Table 8.1 presents a set of indicators that policy-makers can use as a reference point for decision-making.

Table 8.1 Categories of Shadow Education Policy

Conditions for operation	Registration	Educational license Commercial license	
	Premise	Nature: commercial and/or residential	
		Safety	Fire safety (fire escape; level of floors) Staircase handles Hygiene
		Size	Per student area Total area
	Facilities	Teaching equipment	
Daily operation	Student enrolment	Advertising	No false claims or misleading representation
		Scale	Number of students enrolled
		Target groups	Teachers forbidden to tutor their own students
	Finances	Fees	Information disclosure Charging duration Refund
		Special account for tutoring fees	Minimum account balance Monitoring unusual cash flow

(Continued)

Table 8.1 Categories of Shadow Education Policy *(Continued)*

	Curriculum	Goals	Examination orientation (Prohibition)
			Contests preparation (Prohibition)
		Subjects	Number of tutoring subjects
			Academic/non-academic
		Tutoring materials	Qualifications of material developers/publishers
			Evaluation and approval of content
		Assessments	Entrance examinations/ contests (Prohibition)
			Ranking (Prohibition)
		Pace	In line with school curriculum standards
		Homework	Level of difficulty
			Amount/no homework
	Time	Time of day	Curfew
			Out-of-school hours
		Duration	
	Class size		
	Contracts	Model contract	
		Penalty standards for contract cancellation	
	Consumer protection	Privacy protection	
		Complaint feedback	Hotline
Human resources	Tutors	Qualifications	Certificate
			Degree
		Registration	
		Criminal record	No criminal record
			Tutor blacklist
		Working experience	
		Specific criteria on overseas tutors	
	Managers (owners)	Qualifications	
		No criminal record	
		Working experience	
	Staff training and professional development	Pre-service training	
		On-the-job training	
Organisational structure	Governing body		
	Pedagogical Council		

It is important for policies to take account of the diversity of shadow education (Figure 1.1). Companies seem to be easier to regulate than informal providers and even teachers who provide tutoring. These other tutoring providers should not be neglected, however, because they still deal with children and exert economic, social and educational impact. Among companies, different regulations may be needed for different types of enterprise. For example, different requirements may be needed for online and face-to-face companies; and for-profit enterprises may be treated differently from not-for-profit ones. Also, the enactment of regulations may require attention to the location of activities. Thus, regulation of companies that operate nationally will require coordination across local governments, as shown in the Chinese case. For companies that operate internationally, authorities can insist on national regulations while needing to be aware of further complexities that arise from taxation requirements, employment contracts and other domains that vary in different jurisdictions.

At the other end of the scale from the national and international operators are self-employed tutors. Regulators in Japan and the Republic of Korea, for example allow self-employed tutors to operate under a different framework from larger enterprises.

Elaborating on the modes of tutoring, regulations for offline tutoring may not apply easily to online and dual-tutor models. New emerging modes need research-informed tailor-made policies, which may also take account of seasonal variations in tutoring. In China, the ban on academic tutoring in the summer and winter holidays was followed by frequent inspections and site checks by local authorities during such seasons.

Beyond these practical issues, one further question needs confrontation. Some analysts (e.g. Sutton Trust, 2019; Gordon Györi, 2020) have recommended introduction of vouchers for low-income families so that they are not so strongly disadvantaged in the competition with higher-income families. However, this notion introduces conceptual problems in addition to the practical challenges. Vouchers further strengthen the legitimacy of private tutoring, implying that most – perhaps all – students ought to receive tutoring either paid by their families or by the government.

Takeaway 3: Shadow education and schooling must be considered together

Because shadow education and schooling are intertwined, the two entities must be considered together (see Figure 8.1). Each side shapes the other, and failure to coordinate in policy matters results in pitfalls on both sides.

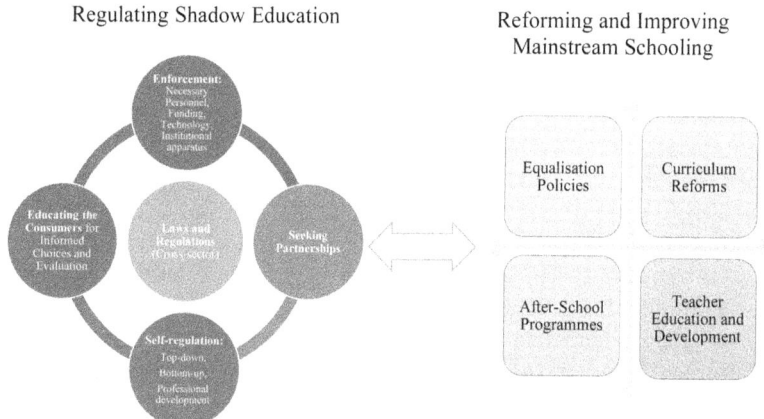

Figure 8.1 An Expanded Conceptual Framework for Regulating Shadow Education

An example of these pitfalls at the macro-level concerns the Education for All (EFA) agenda championed by UNESCO (2000). As noted by Bray (2017), the EFA agenda sought to improve equity by expanding access yet inadvertently stimulated the expansion of shadow education. This was especially evident in Africa, where the expansion of schooling threatened its quality and constrained teachers' salaries (Bray, 2021b). Some families felt a need for private supplementary tutoring in the context of qualitative decline; and many teachers who felt pressure to secure additional incomes to meet their family needs viewed private tutoring as an obvious way to do so. A further factor arising from the successes of universal primary education was pressure for universal junior secondary education and then much expanded senior secondary and higher education. Expansion at these levels further stretched financial and human resources, with implications for quality; and in the competitive environment for limited high-status schools, universities and then jobs, increasing numbers of families felt the need for shadow education to supplement the school sector. Thus, efforts to equalise and expand access to schooling can unintentionally increase the demand for tutoring and expansion of the shadow sector.

Another perspective concerns curriculum. As shown in the cycle of interactions between schooling and shadow education in Japan and China, a side effect when authorities in both countries cut school hours and changed school curricula in order to alleviate study burdens was the expansion of tutoring. The governments in both countries later put back some of the hours through after-school programmes (and Japan also put back some of the curriculum difficulty). These examples show that curriculum reforms should consider education as a whole, with both schooling and shadow education in addition to other avenues for learning.

Analysis in Chapter 3 highlights the blurring boundaries of after-school programmes in schooling. Some ASPs might help reduce inequality and improve student performance, but unregulated PPPs with tutoring providers can lead to negative consequences. In settings where teachers work as tutors, it is important for teacher education and development to confront the dual identity of teacher-tutors and to engage teachers in critical inquiry of the phenomenon. Insofar as tutors also play important roles in the lives and learning of students, tutors need to be qualified and to develop professionally as teachers. Policy on teacher education and professional development should not create an opposition between teachers and tutors. Rather, it should include tutors, not only for them to train and qualify, but also to learn from their experiences and creativity. Therefore, planning of schooling should go hand in hand with regulating and planning of shadow education.

Returning to the African picture, Bray's (2021b) study did note diversity around the continent. Shadow education enrolment rates in Egypt and Mauritius, for example were much higher than those in Lesotho and Namibia. The danger then arises of policy makers in the countries with lower shadow enrolment rates neglecting the matter until it becomes more serious. As with the health sector, and most obviously COVID-19, it is much wiser to act in a preventative way when the challenges are modest than to wait until the point at which structures and habits have already been formed and can only be changed with sorts of drastic measures attempted in the Republic of Korea during the 1980s and in China in 2021.

Expanding the regulatory framework in Figure 1.2, each of these dimensions can be elaborated and revised in the light of global policy progress analysed in this report. Figure 8.1 provides a conceptual framework for policy coordination and integration: as school reforms should go hand in hand with tutoring regulations, all policies for the shadow education sector should also take account of the school sector. The set of square boxes shows only four domains of school-related reform discussed in this report, and in principle the diagram could be modified to include many more domains.

Takeaway 4: Partnerships should go beyond the modes of commercial trade

While international evidence highlights many negative dimensions of tutoring, its diversity and flexibility can foster positive educational innovations and help meet social needs. Tutoring programmes subsidised by the government can be useful for reducing financial gaps, but should also be treated with care, as evidenced in Sweden and England. Comparative analysis in this study has shown that partnerships may take the form of outsourcing, i.e. using public funding to purchase services from tutoring providers. Such partnerships are in effect underpinned by commercial trade, which could lead to unexpected side effects.

Sustainable partnerships are where shadow education, families and school actors coordinate and collaborate towards shared educational goals for student wellbeing and for co-constructing equitable education for all. The author's comparative research in China, Japan, the USA and Denmark has already shown evidence of desirable partnerships beyond contractual relationships. The research shows that innovations in tutoring can empower school transformation and reduce learning gaps. Quality digital resources created by tutoring providers can support schooling, and tutors and teachers can form dynamic and creative professional learning communities.

As UNESCO has shown in its visionary agenda for the future of education (UNESCO, 2021), technological advancement is further dissolving the walls of schools. Thus, schools have to open up, respond to and collaborate with other education providers. In this process, more creative collaboration is needed between state and non-state actors.

COVID-19 has made us stop taking for granted the commitment of state actors and the role of schooling, but it also alerted us of the limitations of the state actors and schooling. The future of education is one with blurred boundaries, of openness of education beyond the myth of schooling. Of course, the transformation of education requires the joint efforts of all parties involved. Problems associated with shadow education cannot be attributed to the industry alone: they also mirror fundamental issues in both schooling and the wider society. Here a core message of UNESCO's 2017/18 GEM Report may be recalled: "Stop the blame game: Education is a shared responsibility" (UNESCO, 2017b, p. 12).

8.4 Summary

The title of this book used the metaphor of a wild horse. Certainly, the horse is more wild in some countries than others, but to some extent, it is wild everywhere – even in Denmark which is otherwise a rather sedate, gentle and regulated society. In some countries, the horse has been wild for some time – in Egypt, for example and also in such countries as Greece and Mauritius. In other countries, again citing Denmark and other Scandinavian countries, the horse is younger.

Historically, schools were also wild; but the history of the 20th century includes a history of taming the schools, bringing regulation even to private institutions to fit with public ones and serve the wider societies. The shadow sector has received less attention, and the book as a whole argues that it needs more attention. This is a summary of the whole book rather than just this chapter; but the chapter indeed shows that much can be learned from comparing.

Appendix

Appendix 1: Scale of Private Supplementary Tutoring in Selected Countries and Jurisdictions

Country	Patterns
Argentina	Cámara and Gertel (2016) surveyed 360 freshmen at the University of Córdoba. They found that 17.5% of students in Law had received private tutoring before their admission to the university, and the figures for those in Dentistry, Economic and Medicine were 30.9%, 39.2% and 92.4%, respectively (p. 140).
Austria	Data in 2017 indicated that 28% of upper secondary students in the academic (gymnasium) stream had received tutoring in the present or previous year (Boehm, 2018, p. 46).
Azerbaijan	Silova and Kazimzade (2006) asked 913 first-year university students about their experiences in the last year of secondary schooling. They found that 93.0% of students had received tutoring (private lessons, preparatory courses, or both).
Bangladesh	National household survey data showed 2000 private tutoring enrolment rates of 47.7% in urban areas compared with 27.5% in rural areas. The repeat survey in 2010 showed proportions of 66.7% and 53.9% (Pallegedara & Mottaleb, 2018, p. 45). Mahmud and Bray (2017) surveyed 401 students from Grades 8 and 10 in eight secondary schools in two locations on their participation in tutoring in English. They found that the overall participation rate was 71.3%, and the mean of monthly household expenditures on private tutoring was 1,290 Taka.
Brazil	Ventura and Gomes (2013, p. 141) reviewed existing literature and noted that 22.0% of students from public schools and 51.9% from private schools regularly used private tutoring. They added that the average estimated yearly spending in 2008 was US$1,389 for public school students and US$2,456 for private school students.

(Continued)

Appendix 1: Scale of Private Supplementary Tutoring in Selected Countries and Jurisdictions *(Continued)*

Country	Patterns
Canada	Aurini and Davies (2013) reviewed existing literature and found that "33% of Canadian parents have purchased supplementary education, and 21% of 9-year-old children have received some kind of private tutoring" (p. 157). In addition, they found that from the 1990s into the 2000s, the number of tutoring businesses increased rapidly in major Canadian cities (p. 160).
China	The China Education Panel Survey compared patterns before and after the double-burden-reduction policy (Wang, 2021). In the 2021 spring semester, 48.1% of primary and lower secondary students had received academic tutoring, and the figure dropped to 21.7% in the fall semester. Participation rates in non-academic tutoring and home tutoring also dropped – from 50.8% to 38.9%. In terms of online tutoring, a study by the Key Laboratory of Big Data Mining and Knowledge Management (2020b) with a focus on online tutoring drew on 3,316 questionnaires by parents with K-9 children in 37 Tier 1-4 cities and other sources. It showed that 46% of urban K-9 students (i.e. 26 million people) received English tutoring. The market size (for K-9 online English education) was RMB260,000 million in 2020, with 5.8 million consumers and a market penetration rate of 22%. The traditional offline market was reported to have 24 million consumers.
Cambodia	Drawing on a nationally representative dataset, Marshall and Fukao (2019) found that 73% of Grade 8 students had received private tutoring in 2016. Data from the Cambodia Socio-Economic Survey (CSES) showed that the participation rate increased steadily from 2004 to 2015 across most Grades and that in 2015 over 60% of Grades 9–12 students had received shadow education (cited in Marshall & Fukao, 2019). The CSES data for 2017 (National Institute of Statistics, 2018) showed participation rates of 20.1% for primary school students, 57.0% for lower-secondary school students, and 74.7% for upper-secondary school students. On a smaller scale, Bray et al. (2016), with data collected from six secondary schools in Siem Reap Province, found that 74.7% of Grade 9 students and 89.8% of Grade 12 students had received shadow education within the last 12 months. Regarding expenditures, they found that the common cost was 500 riels (US$0.13) per lesson or 10,000 riels (US$2.50) per month per subject, with rates higher in urban than rural areas.
Cyprus	Lamprianou and Lamprianou (2013, p. 40) analysed 2003 and 2009 data for households with children aged 6–18. In 2003, 74% of households indicated that they were paying money for private tutoring, and by 2009 the number was 80%.

(Continued)

Appendix 1: Scale of Private Supplementary Tutoring in Selected Countries and Jurisdictions *(Continued)*

Country	Patterns
Czech Republic	Šť'astný (2016, p. 20) surveyed 1,265 upper secondary students in Prague and a less developed region in the east of the country. In Prague, 47.5% were either receiving individual private lessons or joined preparatory courses for university entrance. In the other region, the proportion was 35.9%.
Germany	Hille et al. (2016, p. 66) analysed data from 4,500 households in 2013. Among primary students, 6% were receiving tutoring while for secondary students 18% were doing so. Among children aged 17, 47% reported that they had received tutoring at least once during their careers. Proportions had grown significantly since 2000.
Hong Kong, China	Bray et al. (2014) surveyed 967 Grade 9 students and 657 Grade 12 students in 16 secondary schools in 2010/11. They found that 53.8% of Grade 9 students and 71.8% of Grade 12 students reported having received some sort of tutoring (p. 29). The median reported cost for a secondary school student was HK$1,570 per month, accounting for around 8.7% of the total monthly income of an average family (p. 30). Concerning gender, 65.6% of surveyed female students received tutoring compared with only 56.8% of males (p. 33). A *China Daily* report (Wang, 2018) stated that in 2015/16 the market sale of private tutoring was HK$4.3 billion. A report by Ipsos (2016) stated there were 1,317 tutoring companies, with 2,051 outlets. Only 10.8% of the companies were chain businesses. The average monthly expenditure on private tutoring for primary school students was HK$599 per person in 2015/2016; and total market sale for them was HK$ 1,365.7 million. The report added that 1,100 tutoring companies, with 1,775 branches, targeted secondary school students, and 11.4% of these companies were chain businesses. It estimated the average monthly expenditure on tutoring for secondary school students at HK$634 per student in 2015/2016, and the total market sale that year was HK$2,899.9 million.
Iran	A survey of 300 high school students in Sanandaj indicated that 61% were receiving private tutoring (Shirbagi et al., 2019, p. 51). Among them, 22% received had tutoring for one year, 13% for two years, 41% for three years, and 16% for four or more years. Over half (64%) received more than four hours of tutoring each week.

(Continued)

Appendix 1: Scale of Private Supplementary Tutoring in Selected Countries and Jurisdictions *(Continued)*

Country	Patterns
Japan	The Yano Research Institute (cited in Owner's Lab, 2019) reported that Japan's *juku* market size in 2017 was 969 billion yen, with annual growth of 0.7%. The one-to-one tutoring market size was 439 billion yen in 2017, and its market share was 45.3%. Official data (Japan, METI 2019) showed that Japan had 46,734 *gakushu juku* in 2018, with 327,500 employees (p. 1), and that revenue was 991.9 billion yen in 2017 (p. 16). Further, a report by Ministry of Education, Culture, Sports, Science and Technology (MEXT) (2019) showed household expenditures on tutoring provided by *gakushu juku* and home tutors for students across education levels in 2018. Annual average expenditures on private tutoring for public and private kindergarteners were 84,000 yen and 148,000 yen, respectively. Those for public and private primary school students were 181,000 yen and 452,000 yen. Those for public and private lower-secondary school students were 375,000 yen and 395,000 yen, and for public and private upper-secondary school students were 380,000 yen and 465,000 yen (calculated based on data from MEXT, 2019).
Kazakhstan	Kalikova and Rakhimzhanova (2009, cited in Bray & Lykins, 2012, p. 5) asked 1,004 first-year university students about their experiences in the last year of secondary schooling and found that 59.9% of students had received tutoring (private lessons, preparatory courses, or both).
Kenya	SACMEQ's national survey indicated that 52.1% of sampled Grade 6 students in 2007 were receiving paid extra tuition and a further 18.1% were receiving fee-free extra tuition (Wasanga et al. 2012, pp. 38–39). The report on the 2013 SACMEQ survey indicated a total of 63.0% receiving extra tuition but did not distinguish between fee-free and fee-charging (Karogo et al., 2019, p. 39). A 2013 survey of 487 students in 31 secondary schools by Getange and Obar (2016, p. 11) showed an enrolment rate of 83.1%.

(Continued)

Appendix 1: Scale of Private Supplementary Tutoring in Selected Countries and Jurisdictions *(Continued)*

Country	Patterns
Korea, Republic of	Total household expenditures on private tutoring were estimated at 24 trillion Korean won or 2.8% of GDP in 2006, equivalent to 80% of government expenditures on public education for primary and secondary education (Kim & Lee, 2010, p. 261). More recent data from Private Education Expenditure Survey conducted by the Korean Statistical Information Service (KOSIS) (2019) showed that in 2019, 57.9% of elementary school students were receiving tutoring of some kind (one-on-one, group, via internet, at home and in private institutes). The figures for lower-secondary and upper-secondary school students were 61.8% and 49.7%. Students with higher monthly household income were more likely to receive private tutoring: 27.6% of students with less than two million won were receiving tutoring, whereas for students who reported "less than 6 to 7 million won a month", the percentage was 66.5%. Average monthly expenditures on private tutoring for families with monthly incomes below two million won was 64,000 won; the expenditure increased for richer families, and for families with monthly income "less than 6 to 7 million won" (the richest families in the Survey), the average monthly spending was 300,500 won. There were no significant differences in participation rates for males (55.1%) and females (58.5%).
Mauritius	A 1986 national survey indicated shadow education enrolment rates of 11.2% in Grade 1, 72.7% in Grade 6, 37.3% in Grade 7 and 87.2% in Grade 12 (Joynathsing et al., 1988, p. 31). SACMEQ data for Grade 6 indicated an 81.4% enrolment rate in 2013 (Dwarkan, 2017, p. 37).
Mozambique	SACMEQ data indicated that 9.7% of sampled Grade 6 students in 2007 were receiving private tutoring. The proportion increased to 20.8% in 2013 (Moreno et al., 2017, p. 48).
Myanmar	Bray, Kobakhidze and Kwo (2020) surveyed 801 Grade 9 and 836 Grade 11 students from eight schools (five urban and three rural) in Yangon Region, asking about their participation in private tutoring during the past 12 months. The overall participation rate was 84.9%, with little variation between genders, grades and locations. For males the figure was 86.4% compared with 84.5% for females; for Grade 9 the figure was 83.4% compared with 86.2% in Grade 11; and for urban students, the figure was 88.2% compared with 79.4% for peri-urban students (p. 41). Mean monthly expenditure on private tutoring was 42,797 Kyats for Grade 9 students, and 100,460 Kyats for Grade 11 students; 80,672 Kyats for urban students, 49,571 Kyats for peri-urban students; 76,277 Kyats for males and 67,223 Kyats for females (p. 44).

(Continued)

Appendix 1: Scale of Private Supplementary Tutoring in Selected Countries and Jurisdictions *(Continued)*

Country	Patterns
Nepal	National household survey data showed 2010 private tutoring enrolment rates of 16.1% among children aged 6–10, 26.1% among ones aged 11–15, and 43.2% among ones aged 16–18 (Dahal & Nguyen, 2014, p. 14).
Pakistan	The Annual Status of Education Report (ASER) collects data separately in rural and urban areas. In 2019, 6% of rural government-school children were receiving private tutoring, and 22% of private-school children were doing so (ASER, 2020, p. 69). The highest rates were in Grade 10, at 11% and 28%. In urban areas in 2018, 25% of government-school children were receiving private tutoring, and 45% of private-school children were doing so (ASER, 2019, p. 37). Again the highest rates were in Grade 10, at 42% and 59%; but even in Grade 1 they were 21% and 13%.
Poland	Długosz (2017) surveyed 3,479 school leavers and found that 52.0% had received private lessons. In earlier research, Murawska and Putkiewicz (2006) found that among 849 first-year university students in 2004/05, 49.8% reported having received private lessons.
Qatar	A 2015 survey secured information from 1,298 parents of students in 37 secondary schools (Sellami & Trung, 2020). Among parents of children in Grades 8 or 9, 29.3% indicated that their children received private tutoring. The figure for children in Grades 11 or 12 was 45.0%.
Singapore	A report in *The Straits Times* showed that the number of tutoring and enrichment centres had increased from about 700 in 2012 to over 950 in 2019 (cited in Cheng, 2019). The Household Expenditure Survey 2017/18 conducted by the Singapore Department of Statistics (2019) indicated that households spent SG$1.4 billion on private tutoring that year, increased from SG$1.1 billion in 2012/13 (Cheng, 2019). Average monthly household spending on tutoring was to SG$88 in 2017/18, compared to S$80 in 2012/13 (Cheng, 2019). In 2017/18, for home-based private tutoring, the average monthly expenditure was SG$34, and that for centre-based tutoring was SG$54 (Singapore Department of Statistics, 2019).
South Africa	SACMEQ data indicated that 29.1% of Grade 6 students in 2013 were receiving private tutoring (Chetty et al. 2017, p. 16). This was a considerable increase from the 4.0% recorded in 2007 (Bray, 2021b, p. 17).
Sri Lanka	Pallegedara (2018) drew on Household Income and Expenditure Survey (HIES) data and found that the percentage of households that had expenditures on private tutoring grew from 13.9% (1990/91) to 54.2% (2012/13). The percentage for rural families rose from 9.5% (1990/91) to 51.2 (2012/13), and that for urban families from 22.6% to 63.4%. Monthly expenditures on private tutoring per student increased from 688 rupees in 1990/91

(Continued)

Appendix 1: Scale of Private Supplementary Tutoring in Selected Countries and Jurisdictions *(Continued)*

Country	Patterns
	to 1,285 rupees in 2012/13. Rural families' monthly expenditures on private tutoring increased from 453 to 1,112 rupees, and urban families' spending grew from 688 to 1,285 rupees. Abayasekara (2018), drawing on 2016 HIES data, stated that 65% of urban households and 62% of rural ones had invested in private tutoring.
Thailand	In 1992, 144 tutoring institutions were registered with the government. The number increased to 904 in 2001, and further to 1,964 in 2012 (Lao, 2014). In 2001 the Office of National Education Council reported that 30% of secondary school students received private tutoring nationwide, and that total spending on private tutoring was 3,300 million baht (Sinlarat, 2002, cited in Lao, 2014). The Ministry of Education (Thailand, 2018) recorded 2,422 tutorial centres, 9,899 tutors and 491,538 tutees nationwide in 2016. The Economic Research and Training Center (2011, cited in Lao, 2014) reported aggregate household expenditure of US$666.67 million in 2011.
Trinidad & Tobago	A sample of 801 primary school children found that 5.7% in Standard 1 received private tutoring. Proportions rose in subsequent grades to 7.3%, 25.4%, 68.4% and 88.2% in Standard 5 (Barrow & Lochan, 2012, p. 411).
United Arab Emirates	A 2017/18 national study of 3,929 parents of students in Grades 5, 9, 10 and 12 indicated that 27% of students were receiving tutoring (Rocha & Hamed, 2018, p. 22). Proportions were higher among Emiratis (32%) than non-Emiratis (21%).
United Kingdom	In England and Wales, a 2018 survey of 2,381 students aged 11–16 asked whether they had ever received private or home tutoring. In London, 41% of respondents replied affirmatively, and 27% in the rest of the country did so (Sutton Trust, 2019).
United States	Buchman et al. (2010), drawing on the National Education Longitudinal Study, mapped patterns on the use of SAT/ACT preparation by family income. They found that 15% of the richest families (with annual family incomes over US$50,000) had intensively used private courses, and approximately 10% had hired private tutors. Among other families, 5–10% had used the two forms of SAT/ACT preparation. Reports by the US Department of Education showed that in 2006–07, 3.3 million students were eligible for supplemental education services. Among them, 17% received supplemental tutoring, and from 2003 to 2008 the number of state-approved supplemental education providers tripled from 1,024 to 3,050 (Mori, 2013, p. 198). Other reports (cited by Mori, 2013) showed that in 2004/05 24–28% of eligible Grade 2–5 students received supplemental tutoring. Other proportions were 16% for Grade 1, 12–16% for Grades 6–8, and only 2–4% for eligible high school students.

References

Abayasekara, Ashani (2018): 'Shadow education in Sri Lanka'. Retrieved from 29 April 2022 from https://www.ips.lk/wp-content/uploads/2018/04/PPT_24April.pdf.

Abdel-Moneim, Mohamed Alaa (2021): 'In Search of a School Façade: Explaining the Centrality of Private Tutoring among High-Performing Students in Egypt'. *International Journal of Educational Development*, Vol.83, pp.1–14.

Ahmadova, Mehpara (2015): *Regulating Teacher-Provided Private Supplementary Tutoring in Azerbaijan: Challenges and Possible Response*. MEd dissertation, The University of Hong Kong.

Al-Youm, Al-Masry (2018): 'Draft law to criminalize Egypt's unauthorized private education centers: Minister'. *Egypt Independent*, 28 October. https://www.egyptindependent.com/draft-law-to-criminalize-egypts-unauthorized-private-education-centers-minister/

Altinyelken, Hülya Koşar (2013): 'The Demand for Private Tutoring in Turkey: Unintended Consequences of Curriculum Reform', in Bray, Mark; Mazawi, André E. & Sultana, Ronald (eds.), *Private Tutoring across the Mediterranean: Power Dynamics, and Implications for Learning and Equity*. Rotterdam: Sense Publishers, pp.187–204.

Anangisye, William (2016): 'A Review of the Longstanding Ban on Private Supplementary Tutoring in Tanzania Mainland'. *Papers in Education and Development* [University of Dar es Salaam], No.33–34, pp.1–17.

Ando, Daisaku (2017): 'Cooperation Between Public Education and *Juku*'. Presentation at Policy Forum 'Public-Private Partnerships in Supplementary Education: Sharing Experiences in East Asian Contexts', 9–10 December. Comparative Education Research Centre, The University of Hong Kong.

ASER [Annual Status of Education Report] (2019): *ASER Report 2018: National (Urban)*. Lahore: ASER.

ASER [Annual Status of Education Report] (2020): *ASER Report 2019: National (Rural)*. Lahore: ASER.

Aslam, Monazza & Atherton, Paul (2014): 'The Shadow Education Sector in India and Pakistan: Opening Pandora's Box', in Macpherson, Ian;

References

Robertson, Susan & Walford, Geoffrey (eds.), *Education, Privatisation and Social Justice: Case Studies from Africa, South Asia and South East Asia*. Oxford: Symposium Books, pp.137–158.

Assaad, Ragui & Krafft, Caroline (2015): 'Is Free Basic Education in Egypt a Reality or a Myth?. *International Journal of Educational Development*, Vol.45, No.1, pp.16–30.

Aurini, Janice & Davies, Scott (2013): 'Supplementary Education in a Changing Organizational Field: The Canadian Case', in Aurini, Janice; Davies, Scott & Dierkes, Julian (eds.), *Out of the Shadows: The Global Intensification of Supplementary Education*. Bingley: Emerald, pp.155–170.

Aurini, Janice; Davies, Scott & Dierkes, Julian (eds.) (2013): *Out of the Shadows: The Global Intensification of Supplementary Education*. Bingley: Emerald.

Baker, Jordan (2020): 'Tutors Could Become a Fixture of NSW Schools to Close Education Gap'. *The Sydney Morning Herald*, 10 November. https://www.smh.com.au/national/nsw/tutors-could-become-a-fixture-of-nsw-schools-to-close-education-gap-20201110-p56d9o.html

Ball, Stephen J. (2006): *Education Policy and Social Class: The Selected Works of Stephen J. Ball*. Abingdon: Routledge.

Ball, Stephen J.; Maguire, Meg & Braun, Annette (2012): *How Schools Do Policy: Policy Enactments in Secondary Schools*. London: Routledge.

Barman, Priyanka Deb (2020): 'Stop Private Tuition, or Else Leave Jobs, Tripura Govt Warns School Teachers', *Hindustan Times*, 7 June. https://www.hindustantimes.com/education/stop-private-tuition-or-else-leave-jobs-tripura-govt-warns-school-teachers/story-EpR5NxYRV6OUWh YFecuK1K.html

Barnum, Matt (2020a): 'England is Launching a National Tutoring Program. Could the U.S. Follow Suit?' *Chalkbeat*, 10 August. <seurld>https://www.chalkbeat.org/2020/8/10/21362664/england-national-tutoring-program-us-americorps-congress

Barnum, Matt (2020b): 'Evidence of Learning Loss is Piling Up. Here's How the U.S. Could Design a Tutoring Program to Help'. *Chalkbeat*, 9 December.

Barrow, Dorian A. & Lochan, Samuel N. (2012): 'Supplementary Tutoring in Trinidad and Tobago: Some Implications for Policy Making'. *International Review of Education*, Vol.58, No.2, pp.405–422.

Bhattacharjee, Biswendu (2015): 'Tripura HC Bans Private Tuition by Govt Teachers'. *Times of India*, 5 September. https://timesofindia.indiatimes.com/city/guwahati/Tripura-HC-bans-private-tuition-by-govt-teachers/articleshow/48835038.cms

Bhorkar, Shalini (2021): *Private Tutoring and Mainstream Education Linkages in India: A Political Economy Approach*. PhD thesis, University College London.

Bhorkar, Shalini & Bray, Mark (2018): 'The Expansion and Roles of Private Tutoring in India: From Supplementation to Supplantation'. *International Journal of Educational Development*, Vol.62, pp.148–156.

130 References

Bihar, Government of (2010): *Bihar Coaching Institute (Control & Regulation) Act, 2010*. Patna: Government of Bihar.

Boehm, Jan (2018): 'Supplementary Education'. *Journal of Education in Black Sea Region*, Vol.4, pp.44–52.

Bray, Mark (1999): *The Shadow Education System: Private Tutoring and Its Implications for Planners*. Fundamentals of Educational Planning 61, Paris: UNESCO International Institute for Educational Planning (IIEP). https://unesdoc.unesco.org/ark:/48223/pf0000118486?10=null&queryId=92d8b802-a518-4ed7-98f0-c17fa5c14518

Bray, Mark (2003): *Adverse Effects of Supplementary Private Tutoring: Dimensions, Implications, and Government Responses*. Series: 'Ethics and Corruption in Education'. Paris: UNESCO International Institute for Educational Planning (IIEP). https://unesdoc.unesco.org/ark:/48223/pf0000133039?1=null&queryId=ad4f0c1c-18bc-4f7c-9554-c463d15f5b21

Bray, Mark (2009): *Confronting the Shadow Education System: What Government Policies for What Private Tutoring?* Paris: UNESCO International Institute for Educational Planning (IIEP). https://unesdoc.unesco.org/ark:/48223/pf0000185106?1=null&queryId=c2356c7f-fcf2-42a8-aa2e-b177b4f1a11e

Bray, Mark (2011): *The Challenge of Shadow Education: Private Tutoring and Its Implications for Policy Makers in the European Union*. Brussels: European Commission.

Bray, Mark (2014): 'The Impact of Shadow Education on Student Academic Achievement: Why the Research Is Inconclusive and What can Be Done about it'. *Asia Pacific Education Review*, Vol.15, No.3, pp.381–389.

Bray, Mark (2017): 'Schooling and Its Supplements: Changing Global Patterns and Implications for Comparative Education'. *Comparative Education Review*, Vol.62, No.3, pp.469–491. https://www.journals.uchicago.edu/doi/abs/10.1086/692709

Bray, Mark (2021a): 'Shadow Education in Europe: Growing Prevalence, Underlying Forces, and Policy Implications'. *ECNU Review of Education* [East China Normal University], Vol.4, No.3, pp.442–475. https://journals.sagepub.com/doi/full/10.1177/2096531119890142

Bray, Mark (2021b): *Shadow Education in Africa: Private Supplementary Tutoring and Its Policy Implications*. Hong Kong: Comparative Education Research Centre, The University of Hong Kong. https://cerc.edu.hku.hk/books/shadow-education-in-africa-private-supplementary-tutoring-and-its-policy-implications/

Bray, Mark (2021c): 'Swimming Against the Tide: Comparative Lessons from Government Efforts to Prohibit Private Supplementary Tutoring Delivered by Regular Teachers'. *Hungarian Educational Research Journal*, Vol.11, No.2, pp.168–188.

Bray, Mark & Hajar, Anas (2023): *Shadow Education in the Middle East: Private Supplementary Tutoring and Its Policy Implications*. London: Routledge.

Bray, Mark; Kobakhidze, Nutsa & Kwo, Ora (2020): *Shadow Education in Myanmar: Private Supplementary Tutoring and Its Implications for*

Policy Makers. Paris: UNESCO and Hong Kong: Comparative Education Research Centre, The University of Hong Kong.

Bray, Mark, Kobakhidze, Nutsa; Junyan, Liu & Wei, Zhang (2016): 'The Internal Dynamics of Privatised Public Education: Fee-Charging Supplementary Tutoring Provided by Teachers in Cambodia'. *International Journal of Educational Development*, Vol.49, pp.291–299.

Bray, Mark & Kwo, Ora (2014): *Regulating Private Tutoring for Public Good: Policy Options for Supplementary Education in Asia*. Hong Kong: Comparative Education Research Centre, The University of Hong Kong, and Bangkok: UNESCO. https://cerc.edu.hku.hk/books/regulating-private-tutoring-for-public-good-policy-options-for-supplementary-education-asia/

Bray, Mark & Lykins, Chad (2012): *Shadow Education: Private Tutoring and Its Implications for Policy Makers in Asia*. Mandaluyong City: Asian Development Bank, and Hong Kong: Comparative Education Research Centre, The University of Hong Kong.

Bray, Mark; Zhan, Shengli; Lykins, Chad; Wang, Dan & Kwo, Ora (2014): 'Differentiated Demand for Private Supplementary Tutoring: Patterns and Implications in Hong Kong Secondary Education'. *Economics of Education Review*, Vol.38, No.1, pp.24–37.

Bray, Mark & Zhang, Wei (2018): 'Public-Private Partnerships in Supplementary Education: Sharing Experiences in East Asian Contexts'. *International Journal for Research on Extended Education*, Vol.6, No.1, pp.98–106.

Buchmann, Claudia; Condron, Dennis J. & Roscigno, Vincent J. (2010): 'Shadow Education, American Style: Test Preparation, the SAT and College Enrollment'. *Social Forces*, Vol.89, No.2, pp.435–462.

Cámara, Florencia & Gertel, Héctor R. (2016): 'The Shadow Education Market of a Mass Higher Education Institution in Argentina', in Astiz, M. Fernanda & Akiba, Motoko (eds.), *The Global and the Local: Diverse Perspectives in Comparative Education*. Rotterdam: Sense Publishers, pp.133–153.

Carr, Daniel & Wang, Liang Choon (2017): 'The Effect of After-School Classes on Private Tuition, Mental Health and Academic Outcomes: Evidence from Korea'. *Sociology*, Vol.52, No.5, pp.877–897.

Cheng, S.H. (2019). Tuition has Ballooned to a S$1.4b Industry in Singapore. Should We Be Concerned? *Today*, 30 September. Retrieved from https://www.todayonline.com/commentary/tuition-has-ballooned-s14b-industry-singapore-should-we-be-concerned.

Chetty, M., Moloi, M.Q., Poliah, R.R. & Tshikororo, J. (2017): *The SACMEQ IV Project in South Africa: A Study of the Conditions of Schooling and the Quality of Education*. Pretoria: Department of Basic Education.

China, General Office of the State Council (2018): 'Opinions of the General Office of the State Council on Regulating the Development of Private Tutoring Institutions'. Beijing: General Office of the State Council of the People's Republic of China. [in Chinese]

China, General Offices of the Communist Party of China Central Committee and the State Council (2021): 'Further Reducing the Burden of Homework and Out-of-school Tutoring for Compulsory Education Students'. Beijing: General Offices of the Communist Party of China Central Committee and the State Council of the People's Republic of China. [in Chinese]

China, Ministry of Education (MoE) (2000): 'Urgent Notice on Reducing the Heavy Study Burden on Students'. Ministry of Education, Beijing. [in Chinese]

China, Ministry of Education (2008): 'Rules of Professional Ethics of Teachers in Primary and Secondary Schools', Ministry of Education, Beijing. [in Chinese]

China, Ministry of Education (2009): 'Guidance on Regulating and Managing Operations of Primary and Secondary Schools'. Ministry of Education, Beijing. [in Chinese]

China, Ministry of Education (2015): 'Rules on Absolute Prohibition of Primary and Secondary Schools and In-service Teachers from Providing Private Tutoring'. Ministry of Education, Beijing. [in Chinese]

China, Ministry of Education (2018): 'Notice Issued by the General Office of the Ministry of Education on Securing Implementation of the Special Campaign to Rectify Tutoring Institutions'. Beijing: Ministry of Education. [in Chinese]

China, Ministry of Education (2019a): 'National Center for Educational Technology on the Development of the National Online Management Service Platform for Private Tutoring'. Beijing: Ministry of Education. [in Chinese]

China, Ministry of Education [with Cyberspace Administration of China, Ministry of Industry and Information Technology, Ministry of Public Security, State Administration of Radio, Film and Television and National Office of Combating Pornographic and Illegal Publications] (2019b): 'The Ministry of Education Jointly with Other Five Departments on the Implementation of Regulating Online Tutoring'. [in Chinese]

China, Ministry of Education (2020): *Statistical Bulletin of the National Education Development in 2020*, Ministry of Education, Beijing. [in Chinese] Retrieved from http://www.moe.gov.cn/jyb_sjzl/sjzl_fztjgb/202108/t20210827_555004.html

China, Ministry of Education and State Administration for Market Regulation (2020): 'Notice on Focused Rectification of Illegally Using Unfair Terms to Infringe on Consumers' Rights and Interests'. [in Chinese]

China, National Development and Reform Commission [with Ministry of Education and State Administration for Market Regulation] (2021): 'On Strengthening the Supervision of Fees for Academic Tutoring at the Level of Compulsory Education', Beijing. [in Chinese]

China, People's Republic of (2018): 'Notice Issued by the General Offices of Four Ministries including Ministry of Education on a Special Campaign to Rectify Out-of-school Training Institutions to Reduce Extracurricular Study Burden on Primary and Secondary Students'. Beijing: Ministry of Education, Ministry of Civil Affairs, Ministry of Human Resources and

Social Security, and State Administration for Industry and Commerce. [in Chinese]

China, State Education Commission (1994): 'On Fully Implementing the Guiding Education Principles and Reducing the Excessive Study Burden of Primary and Secondary School Students'. Beijing: State Education Commission. [in Chinese]

China, State Education Commission (1995): 'An Urgent Notice on Closing Olympiads Schools (Classes) in all Subjects and at all Levels'. Beijing: State Education Commission. [in Chinese]

Choi, Jaesung & Cho, Rosa Minhyo (2016): 'Evaluating the Effects of Governmental Regulations on South Korean Private Cram Schools'. *Asia Pacific Journal of Education*, Vol.36, No.4, pp.599–621.

Christensen, Søren; Grønbek, Thomas & Bækdahl, Frederik (2021): 'The Private Tutoring Industry in Denmark: Market Making and Modes of Moral Justification'. *ECNU Review of Education* [East China Normal University], Vol.4, No.3, pp.520–545.

Christensen, Søren & Zhang, Wei (2021): 'Shadow Education in the Nordic Countries: An Emerging Phenomenon in Comparative Perspective'. *ECNU Review of Education* [East China Normal University], Vol.4, No.3, pp.431–441.

Coughlan, Sean (2019): 'Quarter of Secondary Pupils "Get Private Tuition"'. *BBC News*, 26 September. https://www.bbc.com/news/education-49826715

Davis, Jenny (2013): *Educational Legitimation and Parental Aspiration: Private Tutoring in Perth, Western Australia*. PhD thesis, University of Western Australia.

Dawson, Walter (2009): 'The Tricks of the Teacher: Shadow Education and Corruption in Cambodia', in Heyneman, Stephen P. (ed.), *Buying Your Way into Heaven: Education and Corruption in International Perspective*. Rotterdam: Sense Publishers, pp.51–74.

Dahal, M. & Nguyen, Q. (2014): *Private Non-State Sector Engagement in the Provision of Educational Services at the Primary and Secondary Levels in South Asia: An Analytical Review of its Role in School Enrollment and Student Achievement*. Policy Research Working Paper 6899. Washington DC: The World Bank.

Daley, Ashley (2020): 'Parents Rushing to Hire Tutors, Teachers to Keep Kids Learning and Engaged, While Not in School', *WCNC News*, 15 July. https://www.wcnc.com/article/news/education/parents-rushing-to-hire-tutors-teachers-to-keep-kids-learning-and-engaged-while-not-in-school/275-9b7d75a5-d103-495d-b7a3-8b0f88a0fc5b, accessed 21 July 2020.

Dhall, Mohan (2020): Interview by Australian Broadcasting Corporation, 'Tutoring: Students Finding a Leading Advantage'. 30 October. https://www.abc.net.au/radio/programs/nightlife/tutoring/12835644

Dierkes, Julian (2011): 'Jukucho as Education Consultants'. *Jukupedia*. 9 September. https://blogs.ubc.ca/jukupedia/category/juku-in-japan/relation-with-schools/

Długosz, Piotr (2012): 'Korepetycje maturazystów pogranicza w latach 2008-2011' [Private Lessons and the Influence of the Matura Examination 2008-2011]'. *Kulturai Edukacja*, Vol.2, No.88, pp.89–106. [in Polish]

Dooley, Karen; Liu, Liwei Livia & Yin, Yue Melody (2020): 'Supplying Private Tuition: Edu-Business and Asian Migration in Australia'. *Discourse: Studies in the Cultural Politics of Education*, Vol.41, No.1, pp.98–109.

Dwarkan, L. (2017): *SACMEQ IV Study Mauritius: A Study of the Conditions of Schooling and the Quality of Education*. Port Louis: Southern and Eastern Africa Consortium for Monitoring Educational Quality (SACMEQ).

Economic Research and Training Center (2011): *Taxation of Private Tutoring in Thailand*. Bangkok: Office of the National Education Council.

Education Endowment Foundation (2020): 'National Tutoring Programme: Supporting Schools to Address the Impact of Covid-19 Closures on Pupils' Learning'. https://educationendowmentfoundation.org.uk/covid-19-resources/national-tutoring-programme/?nsukey=zgaM2UR7sEBKi9W9f0IECcQoWhGEQYT19%2F0LVscCNSPFZ6fQcr5cyhi2v1j%2FjfneuliHPxmNzKXyy6j5EEZ1KuTKu3FDYjTw1TK1dfSJhBUG52Pt9OPnyR3JyvdDf44Z0cR11WXYidTIBi%2BvzmCj3yj%2FGOLaoQg2cKVr2DGxfGPiGy0C0W38xShbvmFPSS0ufTZEUkHFvDf2qYGjt3vERA%3D%3D, accessed 24 July 2020.

Entrich, Steve R. (2018): *Shadow Education and Social Inequalities in Japan: Evolving Patterns and Conceptual Implications*. Cham: Springer.

Entrich, Steve R. (2020): 'Worldwide Shadow Education and Social Inequality: Explaining Differences in the Socioeconomic Gap in Access to Shadow Education across 63 Societies'. *International Journal of Comparative Sociology*, Vol.61, No.6, pp.441–475.

Egypt, Ministry of Education (1947): 'The Organisation of Private [Supplementary] Lessons for Students'. Ministerial Circular No.7530. Cairo: Ministry of Education. [in Arabic]

Egypt, Ministry of Education (1998): 'Banning Private Tutoring'. Ministerial Decree 592/1998. Cairo: Ministry of Education. [in Arabic] https://docs.google.com/viewer?a=v&pid=sites&srcid=ZGVmYXVsdGRvbWFpbnxuYXNyZWxudWJhdGVhY2hlcnNuYW1lc3xneDozNTYzMWM4OTIwMGFFkYTE0

Egypt, Office of the Prime Minister (2013): 'Prime Minister Decision No.428 of 2013'. Cairo: Office of the Prime Minister. http://www.laweg.net/Default.aspx?action=ViewActivePages&ItemID=84082&Type=6

Egypt Independent (2021): 'Egypt's Tax Authority Calls on Private Tutors to Pay Their Taxes'. 5 November. https://egyptindependent.com/egypts-tax-authority-calls-on-private-tutors-to-pay-their-taxes/

El Baradei, Leila (2022): 'Public Service Delivery: Egypt's Pre-University Education Reforms Continuing Through the Pandemic', in Ali, Hamid E. & Bhuiyan, Shahjahan (eds.), *Institutional Reforms, Governance, and Services Delivery in the Global South*. Cham: Palgrave Macmillan, pp.241–263.

El Watan (2015): 'El Sharqia Governor Vows: Close Private Tutorial Centres and Fine their Owners 50,000 Pounds'. *El Watan*, 2 November. [in Arabic] https://www.elwatannews.com/news/details/830320

Fergany, Nader (1994): *Survey of Access to Primary Education and Acquisition of Basic Literacy Skills in Three Governorates of Egypt*. Cairo: UNICEF; and Almishkat Centre for Research and Training.

Folmar, Ruth (2020): *The Revolutionary Classroom: Education and State Building in Nasserist Egypt, 1952-1967*. Dissertation for History Program, The University of Texas at Austin.

Foondun, Raffick (1992): *Private Tuition in Mauritius: The Mad Race for a Place in a 'Five-Star' Secondary School*. Paris: UNESCO International Institute for Educational Planning (IIEP).

Foondun, Raffick (2002): 'The Issue of Private Tuition: An Analysis of the Practice in Mauritius and Selected South-East Asian Countries'. *International Review of Education*, Vol.48, No.6, pp. 485–515.

Galvão, Fernando Vizotto (2020): 'Ensino Suplementar No Contexto Brasileiro: Uma Análise Baseadanos Dados Do ENEM'. *Educação e Sociedade*, Vol.42, pp.1–18.

Getange, Kennedy N. & Obar, Elly Ochieng (2016): 'Implications of Private Supplementary Tuition on Students' Academic Performance in Secondary Education in Awendo Sub-County, Migori County, Kenya'. *International Journal of Novel Research in Education and Learning*, Vol.3, No.3, pp.5–21.

Ghosh, Pubali & Bray, Mark (2020): 'School Systems as Breeding Grounds for Shadow Education: Factors Contributing to Private Supplementary Tutoring in West Bengal, India'. *European Journal of Education*, Vol.55, No.3, pp.342–360.

Goa, Government of (2001): *Goa Coaching Classes (Regulation) Act, 2001*. Panaji: Department of Law and Judiciary.

Goldstein, Michael & Paulle, Bowen (2020) 'Vaccine-Making's Lessons for High-Dosage Tutoring: A Respectful Disagreement about Research'. Fordham Institute, 12 November. https://fordhaminstitute.org/national/commentary/vaccine-makings-lessons-high-dosage-tutoring-respectful-disagreement-about

Gordon Györi, János (2020): 'Árnyékoktatás: Alapfogalmak, kutatás, lehetőségek' [Shadow Education: Basic Concepts, Research, Opportunities]'. *Educatio*, Vol.29, No.2, pp.171–187. [in Hungarian]

Goyal, Yugank (2019): 'A Policy to Regulate Coaching Centres'. *The Hindu*, 28 June. https://www.thehindu.com/opinion/op-ed/a-policy-to-regulate-coaching-centres/article28191289.ece

Guill, Karin; Lüdtke, Oliver & Köller, Olaf (2020): 'Assessing the Instructional Quality of Private Tutoring and Its Effects on Student Outcomes: Analyses from the German National Educational Panel Study'. *British Journal of Educational Psychology*, Vol.90, pp.282–300.

Gupta, Achala (2022): 'Social Legitimacy of Private Tutoring: An Investigation of Institutional and Affective Educational Practices in India'. *Discourse: Studies in the Cultural Politics of Education*, Vol.43, No.4, pp.571–584.

Hajar, Anas & Karakus, Mehmet (2022): 'A Bibliometric Mapping of Shadow Education Research: Achievements, Limitations, and the Future'. *Asia Pacific Education Review*, Vol.23, pp.341–359.

Hallsén, Stina (2021): 'The Rise of Supplementary Education in Sweden: Arguments, Thought Styles, and Policy Enactment'. *ECNU Review of Education* [East China Normal University], Vol.4, No.3, pp.476–493. https://journals.sagepub.com/doi/full/10.1177/2096531120952096

Hartmann, Sarah (2008): *The Informal Market of Education in Egypt: Private Tutoring and its Implications*. Working Paper 88, Mainz: Department of Anthropology and African Studies, Johannes Gutenberg University.

Hartmann, Sarah (2013): 'Education 'Home Delivery' in Egypt: Private Tutoring and Social Stratification', in Bray, Mark; Mazawi, André E. & Sultana, Ronald G. (eds.), *Private Tutoring across the Mediterranean: Power Dynamics, and Implications for Learning and Equity*. Rotterdam: Sense, pp.57–75.

Herrera, Linda (2022): *Educating Egypt: Civic Values and Ideological Struggles*. Cairo: The American University in Cairo Press.

Hille, Adrian; Spie, C. Katarina & Staneva, Mila (2016): *More and More Students, Especially Those from Middle-Income Households, Are Using Private Tutoring*. Berlin: Deutches Institut für Wirtschaftsforschung.

Hindustan Times (2017): '50 Deaths in 60 Days: Are Coaching Centres Driving Students to Suicide?', 22 October. https://www.hindustantimes.com/editorials/50-deaths-in-60-days-are-coaching-centres-driving-students-to-suicide/story-eVmULTaYCUDi4Gdbry4MSI.html

Høgedahl, Laust & Ibsen, Flemming (2017): 'New Terms for Collective Action in the Public Sector in Denmark: Lessons Learned from the Teacher Lock-Out in 2013'. *Journal of Industrial Relations*, Vol.59, No.5, pp.593–610.

Hong Kong, Education Bureau (2012): 'Education (Exemption) (Private Schools Offering Non-Formal Curriculum) Order (Cap. 279F)'. Hong Kong: Education Bureau, Government of the Hong Kong Special Administrative Region.

Hong Kong, Legislative Council Panel on Education (2003): 'Changes in the Regulatory Control of Private Schools Offering Non-Formal Curriculum'. Paper No. CB(2)312/03-04(01). Hong Kong: Legislative Council Panel on Education. Available on http://www.edb.gov.hk/attachment/en/edu-system/other-edu-training/non-formal-curriculum/ed1117cb2-312-1e.pdf, accessed 13 June 2020.

Hua, Haiyan (1996): *Which Students are Likely to Participate in Private Lessons or School Tutoring in Egypt? (A Multivariate Discriminant Analysis)*. EdD dissertation, Harvard University.

Husband, Terry & Hunt, Carolyn (2015): 'A Review of the Empirical Literature on No Child Left Behind from 2001 to 2010'. *Planning and Changing*, Vol.46, No.1/2, pp.212–254.

Ille, Sebastian & Peacey, Mike W. (2019): 'Forced Private Tutoring in Egypt: Moving Away from a Corrupt Social Norm'. *International Journal of Educational Development*, Vol.66, pp.105–118.

India Legal (2019): 'No Regulation Governing Safety in Delhi's Coaching Centres, Says Fire Department'. 19 September. https://www.indialegallive. com/constitutional-law-news/courts-news/no-regulation-governing-safety-delhis-coaching-centres-says-fire-department

India, Ministry of Corporate Affairs (2013): *Companies Act*. New Delhi: Ministry of Corporate Affairs. https://www.mca.gov.in/Ministry/pdf/CompaniesAct2013.pdf

India, Ministry of Human Resource Development (1986): *National Policy on Education*. New Delhi: Ministry of Human Resource Development.

India, Ministry of Human Resource Development (1992): *National Policy on Education 1986: Programme on Action 1992*. New Delhi: Ministry of Human Resource Development. https://www.mhrd.gov.in/sites/upload_files/mhrd/files/upload_document/npe.pdf

India, Ministry of Human Resource Development (2020): *National Education Policy*. New Delhi: Ministry of Human Resource Development. http://niepid.nic.in/nep_2020.pdf

India, Ministry of Law and Justice (2009): *The Right of Children to Free and Compulsory Education Act, 2009*. The Gazette of India, Part II, Section I, No.39.

India, National Statistical Office (2020): *Household Social Consumption on Education in India: NSS 75th Round, July 2017-June 2018*. New Delhi: National Statistical Office, Ministry of Statistics and Programme Implementation. http://www.mospi.gov.in/sites/default/files/NSS75252E/KI_Education_75th_Final.pdf

Ipsos (2016): 'Industry overview'. Retrieved 11 December 2020 https://www1.hkexnews.hk/listedco/listconews/gem/2016/1202/a8484/ege-20160715-14.pdf

Iqbal, Mohammed (2018): 'The Dark Side of Kota's Dream Chasers'. *The Hindu*, 29 December. https://www.thehindu.com/news/national/the-dark-side-of-kotas-dream-chasers/article25861203.ece

Iraq, Ministry of Education (2017a): 'Summary of Conditions for Opening a Private Institute'. Baghdad: Ministry of Education. [in Arabic]

Iraq, Ministry of Education (2017b): 'The Subject of Private Tutoring'. Circular to Directors of Education in all Districts. Baghdad: Ministry of Education. [in Arabic]

Isashiki, Masataka (2017): 'The Relationship Between Government and Private Supplementary Education (*Juku*) in Japan'. Presentation at Policy Forum 'Public-Private Partnerships in Supplementary Education: Sharing Experiences in East Asian Contexts', 9-10 December. Comparative Education Research Centre, The University of Hong Kong.

Japan, Government (1962): *Act against Unjustifiable Premiums and Misleading Representations* (Act No. 134 of May 15), Tokyo. [in Japanese]

Japan, Government (1976): *Act on Specified Commercial Transactions* (Act No. 57), Tokyo. [in Japanese]

Japan, Government (1993): *Unfair Competition Prevention Act*, Tokyo. [in Japanese]

Japan, Government (2000): *Consumer Contract Act* (Act No. 61 of May 12). Tokyo. [in Japanese]

Japan, Government (2003): *Act on the Protection of Personal Information* (Act No. 57 of May 30), Tokyo. [in Japanese]

Japan, Ministry of Economy, Trade and Industry (METI) (2013): Survey of Specified Service Industries 2013 (Official Report). Retrieved from https://www.meti.go.jp/statistics/tyo/tokusabizi/result-2/h25.html [in Japanese]

Japan, Ministry of Economy, Trade and Industry (METI) (2019): Survey of Specified Service Industries 2018 (Official Report). Retrieved from https://www.meti.go.jp/statistics/tyo/tokusabizi/result-2/h30.html. and https://www.meti.go.jp/statistics/tyo/tokusabizi/result-2/h30/pdf/h30outline.pdf [in Japanese]

Japan, Ministry of Education, Culture, Sports, Science and Technology [MEXT] (2008): National Report on the Out-of-school Learning Activities of Children. Retrieved from: http://www.mext.go.jp/b_menu/houdou/20/08/08080710.htm [in Japanese]

Japan, Ministry of Education, Culture, Sports, Science and Technology [MEXT] (2014): Creation of Education Environment after School and on Saturday to Enrich Children's Learning. Retrieved from: https://www.mext.go.jp/component/b_menu/shingi/toushin/__icsFiles/afieldfile/2015/03/16/1355376_1.pdf [in Japanese]

Japan, Ministry of Education, Culture, Sports, Science and Technology [MEXT] (2015): Partnerships between schools and local communities. Tokyo: MEXT. [in Japanese]

Japan, Ministry of Education, Culture, Sports, Science and Technology [MEXT] (2019): Report on household expenditures on education 2018. Retrieved from https://www.mext.go.jp/content/20191212-mxt_chousa01-000003123_01.pdf and https://www.e-stat.go.jp/stat-search/files?page=1&layout=datalist&toukei=00400201&tstat=000001012023&cycle=0&tclass1=000001135827&tclass2=000001135828&tclass3=000001135832&tclass4val=0 [in Japanese]

Japan, Ministry of Education, Culture, Sports, Science and Technology [MEXT] (2020): *Implementation and Introduction of Partnerships between the Community and School in 2020*. Retrieved from: https://manabi-mirai.mext.go.jp/document/chosa/post-10.html [in Japanese]

Jayachandran, Seema (2014): 'Incentives to Teach Badly: After-School Tutoring in Developing Countries'. *Journal of Development Economics*, Vol.108, pp.190–205.

Joshi, Priyadarshani (2021): 'Private Schooling and Tutoring at Scale in South Asia', in Sarangapani, Padma M. & Pappu, Rekha (eds.), *Handbook of Education Systems in South Asia*. Singapore: Springer, pp.1127–1146.

Joynathsing, M.; Mansoor, M.; Nababsing, V.; Pochun, M. & Selwyn, P. (1988): *The Private Costs of Education in Mauritius*. Réduit: School of Administration, University of Mauritius.

Kale, Pratima (1970): 'The Guru and the Professional: The Dilemma of the Secondary School Teacher in Poona, India'. *Comparative Education Review*, Vol.14, No.3, pp.371–376.

Kalikova, Saule & Zhanar Rakhimzhanova (2009): 'Private Tutoring in Kazakhstan', in Silova, Iveta (ed.), *Private Supplementary Tutoring in Central Asia: New Opportunities and Burdens*. Paris: UNESCO International Institute for Educational Planning (IIEP), pp. 93–118.

Kannangara, C.W.W. (1943): *Report of the Special Committee on Education: Sessional Paper XXIV of 1943 Compiled under the Chairmanship of Dr. C.W.W. Kannangara*. Colombo: Government Printer.

Kany, Nicklas (2021): 'The Rise of Private Tutoring in Denmark: An Entrepreneur's Perspectives and Experiences'. *ECNU Review of Education* [East China Normal University], Vol.4, No.3, pp.630–639.

Karlsson, Marie (2021): 'A Question of Time and Place: Student Tutors' Narrative Identities in For- and Non-Profit Contexts in Sweden'. *Compare: A Journal of Comparative and International Education*, Vol.51, No.8, pp.1241–1256.

Karogo, Mercy G.;, Matei, Asumpta; Kipchirchir, Musa; Kawira, Doreen & Omunyang'oli, Patricia (2019): *The SACMEQ IV Project in Kenya: A Study of the Conditions of Schooling and the Quality of Education*. Nairobi: Kenya National Examinations Council.

Kassotakis, Michael & Verdis, Athanasios (2013): 'Shadow Education in Greece: Characteristics, Consequences and Eradication Efforts', in Bray, Mark; Mazawi, André E. & Sultana, Ronald (eds.), *Private Tutoring across the Mediterranean: Power Dynamics, and Implications for Learning and Equity*. Rotterdam: Sense Publishers, pp.93–113.

Kazakhstan, Ministry of Education and Science (2013): Order of the Minister of Education and Science of the Republic of Kazakhstan No.228 of June 14, 2013 "On Approval Model Regulations for Supplementary Institutions for Children". Astana: Ministry of Education and Science of the Republic of Kazakhstan. [in Russian]

Kenayathulla, Husaina Banu (2013): 'Shadow Education in Malaysia'. Presentation at the Policy Forum on *Regulating the Shadow Education System: Private Tutoring and Government Policies in Asia*, 8-9 April. Hong Kong: Comparative Education Research Centre, The University of Hong Kong.

Key Laboratory of Big Data Mining and Knowledge Management (2020a): 'China's K-12 Online Education Market and Consumer Behavior Report'. [in Chinese] Retrieved July 12, 2022, from https://bdk.ucas.ac.cn/index.php/kycg/fxbg/2793-k12.

Key Laboratory of Big Data Mining and Knowledge Management. (2020b). China's online teenager and children English education market report 2020. Retrieved July 14, 2022, from https://bdk.ucas.ac.cn/index.php/kycg/fxbg/2791-2020.

Khaydarov, Sherzod (2020): 'Shadow Education in Uzbekistan: Teachers' Perceptions of Private Tutoring in the Context of Academic Lyceums'. *Orbis Scholae*, Vol.14, No.2, pp.81–104.

Kim, Ji-Ha & Park, Daekwon (2010): 'The Determinants of Demand for Private Tutoring in South Korea'. *Asia Pacific Education Review*, Vol.11, No.3, pp.411–421.

Kim, Soyoung & Hong, Sehee (2018): 'The Effects of School Contexts and Student Characteristics on Cognitive and Affective Achievement in South Korea'. *Asia Pacific Education Review*, Vol.19, pp.557–572.

Kim, Sunwoong & Lee, Ju-ho (2010): 'Private Tutoring and Demand for Education in South Korea'. *Economic Development and Cultural Change*, Vol.58, No.2, pp.259–296.

Komiyama, H. (2012a): 'The Definition of *Gakushu-Juku* and Reasons for Existence', in Sato, Y. (ed.), *History: The 100 Years of Juku and 50 Years of Juku Associations*. Tokyo: Private Tutoring Federation, pp.201–217. [in Japanese].

Komiyama, H. (2012b): 'History of *Juku* after WWII and Educational Issues in Japan', in Sato, Y. (ed.), *History: The 100 Years of Juku and 50 Years of Juku Associations*. Tokyo: Private Tutoring Federation, pp.280–317. [in Japanese].

Korea, Ministry of Education (2020a): About the Center for Reporting Illegal Private Tutoring. https://clean-hakwon.moe.go.kr/info/info.do, accessed 20 July 2020.[in Korean]

Korea, Ministry of Education and Korea Education and Research Information Service (KERIS) (2020b): Online Platform for Administrative Service of *Hagwons* and Tutors. https://clean-hakwon.moe.go.kr/info/info. do, accessed 25 July 2020. [in Korean]

Korea Educational Broadcasting System (EBS) (2020) Introduction. https://global.ebs.co.kr/global/main/index;jsessionid=xfdkcrdrkDpKBKAtbayKSoin0cUyJfCjyy573yT3oe7KOaVJVFmIMOw1CZBLdiWx.eemwas03_servlet_engine1, accessed 24 July 2020. [in Korean]

KOSIS [Korean Statistical Information Service] (2020): Participation Rate on Private Education by School Level and Characteristics. http://kosis.kr/eng/statisticsList/statisticsListIndex.do?menuId=M_01_01&vwcd=MT_ETITLE&parmTabId=M_01_01&statId=1963003&themaId=#SelectStatsBoxDiv accessed 23 February 2022.

Kosunen, Sonja; Haltia, Nina; Saari, Juhani; Jokila, Suvi & Halmkrona, Esa (2021): 'Private Supplementary Tutoring and Socio-Economic Differences in Access to Higher Education'. *Higher Education Policy*, Vol.34, pp.949–968.

Kumar, Anil (2017): 'Bihar Govt to Regulate Private Coaching Institutes'. *Hindustan Times*, 1 April. https://www.hindustantimes.com/patna/bihar-govt-to-regulate-private-coaching-institutes/story-yENn9X1eXelmnRhaXARMQO.html

Kuroishi, N. & Takahashi, M. (2009): 'A Study on Collaborations between the Cram-School Industry and Public Education: From Present Circumstances to Future Proposals'. *Comprehensive Studies of Education*, No.2, pp.1–14. [in Japanese]

Lamprianou, Iasonas & Lamprianou, Thekla Afantiti (2013): 'Charting Private Tutoring in Cyprus: A Socio-Demographic Perspective', in Bray,

Mark; Mazawi, André E. & Sultana, Ronald (eds.), *Private Tutoring across the Mediterranean: Power Dynamics, and Implications for Learning and Equity*. Rotterdam: Sense Publishers, pp.29–56.

Lao, Rattana (2014): 'Analyzing the Thai State Policy on Private Tutoring: The Prevalence of the Market Discourse'. *Asia Pacific Journal of Education*, Vol.34, No.4, pp.476–491.

Lapidus, John (2019): *The Quest for a Divided Welfare State: Sweden in the Era of Privatization*. Cham: Palgrave Macmillan.

Lee, Andrew M.I. (2020): *No Child Left Behind (NCLB): What You Need to Know*. https://www.understood.org/en/school-learning/your-childs-rights/basics-about-childs-rights/no-child-left-behind-nclb-what-you-need-to-know, accessed 28 October 2020.

Lee, Chong Jae; Lee, Heesook & Jang, Hyo-Min (2010): 'The History of Policy Responses to Shadow Education in South Korea: Implications for the Next Cycle of Policy Responses'. *Asia Pacific Education Review*, Vol.11, No.1, pp.97–108.

Lee, Jin (2011): 'The Policies on Supplemental Education in Korea'. *IIAS Newsletter* [International Institute of Asian Studies], No.56, pp.11–12. https://www.iias.asia/sites/default/files/nwl_article/2019-05/IIAS_NL56_1617_0.pdf

Lingard, Bob & Ozga, Jenny (eds.) (2009): *The RoutledgeFalmer Reader in Education Policy and Politics*. London: Routledge.

Lingard, Bob & Sellar, Sam (2013): 'Globalization, Edu-Business and Network Governance: The Policy Sociology of Stephen J. Ball and Rethinking Education Policy Analysis'. *London Review of Education*, Vol.11, No.3, pp.265–280.

Liu, Junyan & Bray, Mark (2017): 'Determinants of Demand for Private Supplementary Tutoring in China: Findings from a National Survey'. *Education Economics*, Vol.25, No.2, pp.205–218.

Loyalka, Prashant & Zakharov, Andrey (2016): 'Does Shadow Education Help Students Prepare for College? Evidence from Russia'. *International Journal of Educational Development*, Vol.49, pp.22–30.

Lu, Chen Yan (2004): 'Teachers' Part-time Employment Outside School Hours'. Director of Personnel, Singapore: Ministry of Education.

Luo, Jiahui & Chan, Cecilia Ka Yuk (2022): 'Influences of Shadow Education on the Ecology of Education: A Review of the Literature'. *Educational Research Review*, Vol.36, pp.1–17.

Macao, Government of (2002): *Administrative Order No.34/2002 on Amending Regulation and License of Private Supplementary Pedagogic Supporting Centres*. Macao: Government Printer. [in Chinese]

Mahdini, Waleed P.D. (2009): 'MoE Comes down Hard on Private Tuitions'. *Borneo Bulletin*, 14 October.

Mahmud, Rafsan (2021): 'Family Socioeconomic Determinants and Students' Demand for Private Supplementary Tutoring in English in Urban and Rural Bangladesh'. *Education and Urban Society*, Vol.54, No.7, pp.831–851.

Mahmud, Rafsan & Bray, Mark (2017): 'School Factors Underlying Demand for Private Supplementary Tutoring in English: Urban and Rural Variations in Bangladesh'. *Asia Pacific Journal of Education*, Vol.37, No.3, pp.229–309.

Malaysia, Government of (2006): 'Guidelines for Approval to do Jobs Outside as Tutors or Part-time Trainers'. Service Circular No.1 of 2006. Putrajaya: Ministry of Education. [in Malay]

Maldives, Ministry of Education (2002): *Guidelines for Teachers*. Male: Ministry of Education.

Majumdar, Manabi (2018): 'Access, Success, and Excess: Debating Shadow Education in India', in Kumar, Krishna (ed.), *Routledge Handbook of Education in India: Debates, Practices, and Policies*. New York: Routledge, pp.273–284.

Manipur, Government of (2017): *The Manipur Coaching Institute (Control and Regulation) Act, 2017*. Imphal: Government of Manipur.

Mariya, Maryam (2012): *'I Don't Learn at School, so I Take Tuition': An Ethnographic Study of Classroom Practices and Private Tuition Settings in the Maldives*. PhD thesis, Massey University.

Marshall, Jeffery H. & Fukao, Tsuyoshi (2019): 'Shadow Education and Inequality in Lower Secondary Schooling in Cambodia: Understanding the Dynamics of Private Tutoring Participation and Provision'. *Comparative Education Review*, Vol.63, No.1, pp.98–120.

Mikhaylova, Tatiana (2022): *Shifting Shadows: Private Tutoring and the Formation of Education in Imperial, Soviet and Post-Soviet Russia*. Uppsala: Acta Universitatis Upsaliensis.

Mikkelsen, Sidse Hølvig & Gravesen, David Thore (2021): 'Shadow Education in Denmark: In the Light of the Danish History of Pedagogy and the Skepticism Toward Competition'. *ECNU Review of Education* [East China Normal University], Vol.4, No.3, pp.546–565.

Moreno, Albertina; Nheze, Ismael; Lauchande, Carlos; Manhica, Glória; Mateus, Celso; Afo, Lúcio; Nahara, Trindade & Magaia, Flávio (2017): *The SACMEQ IV Project in Mozambique: A Study of the Conditions of Schooling and the Quality of Primary Education in Mozambique*. Maputo: National Institute for Education Development.

Moreno Olmedilla, Juan Manuel (2022): 'A Perfect Storm: High-stakes Examination and Private Tutoring in Egypt'. *Revista Española de Educación Comparada*, No.40, pp.146–161.

Mori, Izumi (2013): 'Supplementary Education in the United States: Policy, Context, Characteristics, and Challenges', in Aurini, Janice; Davies, Scott & Dierkes, Julian (eds.), *Out of the Shadows: The Global Intensification of Supplementary Education*. Bingley: Emerald, pp.191–207.

Murawska, Barbara & Putkiewicz, Elżbieta (2006): 'Poland', in Silova, Iveta; Būdienė, Virginija & Bray, Mark (eds.), *Education in a Hidden Marketplace: Monitoring of Private Tutoring*. New York: Open Society Institute, pp.257–277.

National Institute for Research Advancement (NIRA) (1996): *Japanese Education as Seen Through Its Cram Schools*. Tokyo: NIRA. [in Japanese].

Neto-Mendes, António (2008): 'A Regulação das Explicações enter o Estado e o Mercado', in Costa, Jorge Adelino; Neto, Mendes, António & Ventura, Alexandre (eds.), *Xplika: Investigaçao sobre o Mercado das Explicações*. Aveiro: Universidade de Aveiro, pp.85–102.

Nguyen, The Cuong; Hafeez-Baig, Abdul; Gururajan, Raj & Nguyen, Nam C. (2021): 'The Hidden Reasons of the Vietnamese Parents for Paying Private Tuition Fees for Public School Teachers'. *Social Sciences & Humanities Open*, Vol.3, pp.1–10.

Odisha, Government of (2017): *Bill for Regulation of Coaching Institutes/ Centres*. Bhubaneswar: Government of Odisha.

OpIndia (2018): 'Maharashtra Private Coaching Regulation Act, 2018: Owners of Tuition Centres Claim It's Unfair'. 17 June. https://www.opindia.com/2018/06/maharashtra-private-coaching-regulation-act-2018-owners-of-tuition-centres-claim-its-unfair/

Ostromukhova, Polina Valer'evna (2016): 'The Distinctive Features of the Content of Additional Education for Children in Russia'. *The World of Science*, Vol. 4, No. 2, pp.1–12. http://mir-nauki.com/PDF/46PDMN216.pdf [in Russian]

Owner's Lab (2019): 'Trends of Private Tutoring Industry'. Retrieved 11 December 2020 from https://www.strike.co.jp/ma_trend/education/trend/cramschool_2019_trend.html.

Pakistan, Senate Secretariat (2013): *Act No.XI, to Provide for the Registration, Regulation and Functioning of Private Educational Institutions in Islamabad Capital Territory*. 19 March. Islamabad: The Gazette of Pakistan.

Pallegedara, Asankha (2018): 'Private Tutoring Expenditure: An Empirical Analysis Based on Sri Lankan Households'. *Review of Development Economics*, Vol.22, No.3, pp.1278–1295.

Pallegedara, Asankha & Mottaleb, Khondoker Abdul (2018): 'Patterns and Determinants of Private Tutoring: The Case of Bangladesh Households'. *International Journal of Educational Development*, Vol.59, pp.43–50.

Park, Hyunjeong; Buchmann, Claudia; Choi, Jaesung & Merry, Joseph J. (2016): 'Learning Beyond the School Walls: Trends and Implications'. *Annual Review of Sociology*, Vol.42, pp.231–252.

Park, Hyunjeong; Byun, Jongim & So, Soonok (2012): 'Do After-School Programs Matter? A Longitudinal Study on the Effectiveness of Participating in After-School Programs in Korea'. *KEDI Journal of Educational Policy*, Vol.9, No.1, pp.3–27.

Patel, Shri Devji M. (2016): *The Private Coaching Centres Regulatory Board Bill, 2016*. Bill No.94 as Introduced in Lok Sabha, New Delhi: Parliament of India. http://164.100.47.4/billstexts/lsbilltexts/asintroduced/38LS.pdf.

Piao, Huiyan (2020) Translation of Selected Tutoring Policies in Korea. Centre for International Research in Supplementary Tutoring, East China Normal University, Shanghai.

Piao, Huiyan & Hwang, Hyuna (2021): 'Shadow Education Policy in Korea During the COVID-19 Pandemic'. *ECNU Review of Education* [East China Normal University], Vol.4, No.3, pp.652–666. https://journals.sagepub.com/doi/full/10.1177/20965311211013825

Psacharopoulos, George & Papakonstantinou, George (2005): 'The Real University Costs in a "Free" Higher Education Country'. *Economics of Education Review*, Vol.24, No.1, pp.103–108.

Punjabi, Shalini (2020): 'Is Shadow Education Becoming the 'New' Formal? Effects of Pedagogical Approaches of IIT-JEE Coaching on School Education in the City of Delhi'. *Contemporary Education Dialogue*, Vol.17, No.1, pp.14–44.

Qureshi, Mehab (2021): 'BYJU's Buys Aakash for $1 Bn: A Look at the Test Prep Co's Journey'. *The Quint*, 8 April. https://www.thequint.com/tech-and-auto/tech-news/byjus-acquires-aakash-educational-services-for-dollar-1-billion#read-more

Rao, S. Srinivasa (2017): 'Production of an "Educational" City: Shadow Education Economy and Re-Structuring of Kota in India', in Pink, William T. & Noblit, George W. (eds.), *Second International Handbook of Urban Education*. Dordrecht: Springer, pp.417–443.

Ridge, Natasha; Shami, Soha & Kippels, Susan (2017): 'Arab Migrant Teachers in the United Arab Emirates and Qatar: Challenges and Opportunities', in Babar, Zahra (ed.), *Arab Migrant Communities in the GCC*. Oxford: Oxford University Press, pp.39–63.

Rocha, Valeria & Hamed, Sheren (2018): *Parents' Perspectives on Paid Private Tutoring in the United Arab Emirates*. Sharjah: UNESCO Regional Center for Educational Planning.

Roesgaard, Marie H. (2006): *Japanese Education and the Cram School Business: Functions, Challenges and Perspectives of the Juku*. Copenhagen: Nordic Institute of Asian Studies Press.

Russian Federation, Government (2013): Decree of the Government of the Russian Federation No. 966 October 28, 2013 "On Licensing of Educational Activities". Moscow: The Government of the Russian Federation. [in Russian]

Russian Federation, Ministry of Education (2018): Order of the Ministry of Education of the Russian Federation on November 9, 2018 No. 196 "On the Approval of the Order of Organization and Implementation of Educational Activities on Supplemental Education Programs". Moscow: Ministry of Health of the Russian Federation. [in Russian]

Russian Federation, Ministry of Health (2014): Sanitary Inspector of the Russian Federation Resolution No. 41 July 4, 2014 "On Implementing Sanitary Rules". Moscow: Ministry of Health of the Russian Federation. [in Russian]

Russian Federation, Ministry of Labour and Social Protection (2018): Order of the Ministry of Labour and Social Protection of the Russian Federation No. 298, May 5, 2018 "On Approval of Professional Standards of Teachers of Supplementary Education for Children and Adults". Moscow: Ministry of Labour and Social Protection of the Russian Federation. [in Russian]

Saavedra, Jaime (2019): 'Shaking up Egypt's Public Education System'. Washington DC: The World Bank. https://blogs.worldbank.org/education/shaking-egypts-public-education-system, accessed 27 April 2022.

Santos, Melissa (2014): 'New Rules will Govern Tutoring Companies operating under No Child Left Behind'. *The News Tribune*, 25 August. https://www.thenewstribune.com/news/local/education/article25878070.html

Sato, Y. (ed.) (2012): *History: The 100 Years of Juku and 50 Years of Juku Associations*. Tokyo: Private Tutoring Federation. [in Japanese]

Sellami, Abdellatif & Trung, Kien Le (2020): 'Predictors of Parental Use of Private Tutoring in Qatar'. *International Journal of Humanities Education*, Vol.18, No.2, pp.17–36.

Sherratt, Fred; Sherratt, Simon & Ivory, Chris (2020): 'Challenging Complacency in Construction Management Research: The Case of PPPs'. *Construction Management and Economics*, Vol.28, No.12, pp.1086–1100.

Shirbagi, Naser; Afshinfar, Jafar; Ghaslani, Rozhin; Sadeghi, Sharareh & Nasirinia, Shahab (2019): 'Luxury Expenses of Shadow Education: A Comparative Study of Iranian Students, Parents and Teachers' Views'. *Iranian Journal of Comparative Education*, Vol.2, No.1, pp.41–64.

Sieverding, Maia; Krafft, Caroline & Elbadawy, Asmaa (2019): 'An Exploration of the Drivers of Private Tutoring in Egypt'. *Comparative Education Review*, Vol.63, No.4, pp.562–590.

Silova, Iveta (2010): 'Private Tutoring in Eastern Europe and Central Asia: Policy Choices and Implications'. *Compare: A Journal of Comparative and International Education*, Vol.40, No.3, pp.327-344.

Silova, Iveta & Kazimzade, Elmina (2006): 'Azerbaijan', in Silova, Iveta; Būdienė, Virginija & Bray, Mark (eds.), *Education in a Hidden Marketplace: Monitoring of Private Tutoring*. New York: Open Society Institute, pp.113–141.

Silova, Iveta; Būdienė, Virginija & Bray, Mark (eds.) (2006): *Education in a Hidden Marketplace: Monitoring of Private Tutoring*. New York: Open Society Institute.

Singapore Department of Statistics (2019): *Household Expenditure Survey 2017/2018*. Retrieved 11 December 2020 from https://www.singstat.gov.sg/publications/households/household-expenditure-survey.

Singapore, Ministry of Education (2019): 'Parliamentary Replies: Tuition'. 7 October.

Sinlarat, P. (2002): *Private Tutoring in Secondary Education in Thailand*. Bangkok: Office of the National Education Council.

Smith, Alexandra (2020): 'Students Get Free Tutoring After Falling Behind During COVID-19 Remote Learning'. *The Sydney Morning Herald*, 10 November. https://www.smh.com.au/national/nsw/students-get-free-tutoring-after-falling-behind-during-covid-19-remote-learning-20201109-p56cy7.html

Sobhy Ramadan, Hania (2012): *Education and the Production of Citizenship in the Late Mubarak Era: Privatization, Discipline and the Construction of the Nation in Egyptian Secondary Schools*. PhD thesis, School of Oriental and African Studies, University of London.

Springborg, Robert (2021): 'Educational Policy in Sisi's Egypt', in Alaoui, Hicham & Springborg, Robert (eds.), *The Political Economy of Education in the Arab World*. Boulder: Lynne Rienner, pp.87–102.

146 References

Šťastný, Vít (2016): Fenomén soukromého doučování jako stínový vzdělávací systém v České republice [*Private supplementary tutoring phenomenon as a shadow education system in the Czech Republic*]. PhD thesis, Charles University, Prague.

Sutton Trust (2019): *Private Tuition Polling 2019*. https://www.suttontrust.com/wp-content/uploads/2019/12/PrivateTuition2019-PollingTables.pdf and https://www.suttontrust.com/news-opinion/all-news-opinion/one-in-four-teachers-take-on-private-tuition-outside-of-school

Tadros, Mariz (2006): 'State Welfare in Egypt Since Adjustment: Hegemonic Control with a Minimalist Role'. *Review of African Political Economy*, Vol.33, No.108, pp.237–254.

Thailand, Ministry of Education (2018): 'Educational Statistics'.

The Hindu (2021): 'Byju's buys Aakash in $940-m cash/stock deal'. 6 April. https://www.thehindubusinessline.com/news/education/byjus-acquires-aakash-educational-services/article34243695.ece

The Times of India (2015): 'Tripura Students, Guardians Bat for pvt Tuition'. 21 June. https://timesofindia.indiatimes.com/city/guwahati/Tripura-students-guardians-bat-for-pvt-tuition/articleshow/47750620.cms

Tomorrow Advancing Life (TAL) (2020): Artificial Intelligence Solutions for Evaluation of Teaching and Learning.

TripuraInfo (2020): 'Government Decision on Private Tuition Provokes Protest from Students and Guardians'. 8 June.

Tunisia, Ministry of Education [Ministère de l'Éducation] (2015): 'Décret gouvernemental n° 2015-1619 du 30 octobre 2015, fixant les conditions d'organisation des leçons de soutien et des cours particuliers au sein des établissements éducatifs publics'. *Journal Officiel de la République Tunisienne*, No.88, 3 Novembre, pp.2641–2643.

Ukraine, Parliament (2000): 'Law of Ukraine since 22 June 2000 No. 1841- on Extracurricular Education'; Revisions to original text on 2 October 2018. Kiev: Ukraine Parliament. [in Russian]

UNESCO (2000): *The Dakar Framework for Action – Education for All: Meeting Our Collective Commitments*. Paris: UNESCO.

UNESCO (2017a): *Unpacking Sustainable Development Goal 4: Education 2030*. Paris: UNESCO.

UNESCO (2021a): *Non-State Actors in Education: Who Chooses? Who Loses?* Global Education Monitoring Report 2021/2. Paris: UNESCO. https://unesdoc.unesco.org/ark:/48223/pf0000379875

UNESCO (2017b): *Accountability in Education: Meeting our Global Commitments*. Global Education Monitoring Report 2017/8. Paris: UNESCO.

UNESCO (2021): *Reimagining Our Futures Together: A New Social Contract for Education*. Paris: UNESCO.

Uttar Pradesh, Government of (2002a): *The Uttar Pradesh Regulation of Coaching Act, 2002*. Lucknow: Government of Uttar Pradesh. http://www.bareactslive.com/ALL/up628.htm#0

Uttar Pradesh, Government of (2002b): *The Uttar Pradesh Regulation of Coaching Rules, 2002*. Lucknow: Government of Uttar Pradesh. http://www.bareactslive.com/ALL/up852.htm#0

Uzbekistan, Cabinet of Ministers (1995): Cabinet of Ministers of the Republic of Uzbekistan Resolution No. 59 February 18, 1995 "On Approval of the Regulations on Educational Institutions Annex No 2 "About Supplementary Education". Tashkent: Cabinet of Ministers of the Republic of Uzbekistan. [in Russian]

Uzbekistan, Ministry of Health (2013): Sanitary Inspector of the Republic of Uzbekistan Resolution No. 0307-13 January 23, 2013 on Implementing Sanitary Rules for Supplementary Education. Tashkent: Ministry of Health of the Republic of Uzbekistan. [in Russian]

Ventura, Alexandre & Gomes, Candido (2013): 'Supplementary Education in Brazil: Diversity and Paradoxes', in Aurini, Janice; Davies, Scott & Dierkes, Julian (eds.), *Out of the Shadows: The Global Intensification of Supplementary Education*. Bingley: Emerald, pp.129–151.

Wang, Jenny (2018): 'Tuition Mills rake in Billions while Children Suffer'. *China Daily*, 30 July.

Wang, Weidong (2021): 'Effective Implementation of "Double Reduction": Returning to the Essence of Education for the Holistic and Healthy Growth of Children'. *Guangming Daily*, 26 October. [in Chinese] https://epaper.gmw.cn/gmrb/html/2021-10/26/nw.D110000gmrb_20211026_1-13.htm

Warsen, Rianne; Nederhand, José; Klijn, Erik Hans; Grotenbreg, Sanne & Koppenjan, Joop (2018): 'What Makes Public-Private Partnerships Work? Survey Research into the Outcomes and the Quality of Cooperation in PPPs'. *Public Management Review*, Vol.20, No.8, pp.1165–1185.

Wasanga, Paul M.; Ogle, Mukhtar A. & Wambua, Richard M. (2012): *The SACMEQ IV Project in Kenya: A Study of the Conditions of Schooling and the Quality of Education*. Nairobi: Kenya National Examinations Council.

Weale, Sally (2018): '"An Education Arms Race": Inside the Ultra-Competitive World of Private Tutoring'. *The Guardian*, 5 December. https://www.theguardian.com/education/2018/dec/05/an-education-arms-race-inside-the-ultra-competitive-world-of-private-tutoring

Weale, Sally & Adams, Richard (2020): 'Government to Fund Private Tutors for English Schools'. *The Guardian*, 17 June. https://www.theguardian.com/education/2020/jun/17/government-to-fund-private-tutors-for-english-schools?fbclid=IwAR0JX6sMNHreQRd3Awl9yAOA5ydaam4O7j_uIiEkcbnkznY9ILhtbnJYyu4

Weale, Sally (2021): 'UK Tutoring Scheme uses under-18s in Sri Lanka Paid as Little as £1.57 an Hour'. *The Guardian*, 19 March. https://www.theguardian.com/education/2021/mar/19/uk-tutoring-scheme-uses-sri-lankan-under-18s-paid-as-little-as-157-an-hour

Wei, Yi (2018): 'Summary Report on the CIEFR-HS Data'. *Educational Finance in China*, Vol.5, pp.1–20. [in Chinese]

Western Australia, Department of Education (2004): 'Working with Children (Criminal Record Checking) Act 2004'. http://det.wa.edu.au/policies/detcms/policy-planning-and-accountability/policies-framework/legislation/working-with-children-criminal-record-checking-act-2004.en

Western Australia, Department of Education (2018): *Private Teachers in Public Schools*. Perth: Department of Education.

The White House (2022): *Fact Sheet: Biden-Harris Administration Launches National Effort to Support Student Success*. Washington DC: The White House. https://www.whitehouse.gov/briefing-room/statements-releases/2022/07/05/fact-sheet-biden-harris-administration-launches-national-effort-to-support-student-success/?utm_content=&utm_medium=email&utm_name=&utm_source=govdelivery&utm_term=

Williamson, Ben & Hogan, Anna (2020): *Commercialisation and Privatisation in/of Education in the Context of Covid-19*. Brussels: Education International.

The World Bank (2018): *Project Appraisal Document on a Proposed Loan in the Amount of US$500 Million to the Arab Republic of Egypt for a Supporting Egypt Education Reform Project*. Washington DC: The World Bank. http://documents.worldbank.org/curated/en/346091522415590465/pdf/PAD-03272018.pdf.

The World Bank (2002): *Arab Republic of Egypt Education Sector Review: Progress and Priorities for the Future*. Vol. 1, Main Report. Washington DC: The World Bank. https://openknowledge.worldbank.org/bitstream/handle/10986/15339/multi0page.pdf?sequence=1&isAllowed=y

Xinhua (2021): 'China Adopts New Law on Family Education Promotion'. *China Daily*, 23 October. https://www.chinadaily.com.cn/a/202110/23/WS61739a5ca310cdd39bc70c96.html

Yamato, Yoko & Zhang, Wei (2017): 'Changing Schooling, Changing Shadow: Shapes and Functions of *Juku* in Japan'. *Asia Pacific Journal of Education*, Vol.37, No.3, pp.329–343.

Yeomans, Emily (2021): 'What can England Learn from International Catch-up Strategies?'. *National Tutoring Programme-Opinion*, 29 January.

Yuuki, M.; Sato, Z. & Hashisako, K. (1987): *Gakushu-Juku: Perspectives from Children, Parents and Teachers*. Tokyo: Gyosei. [in Japanese]

Zhang, Wei (2013): Private Supplementary Tutoring Received by Grade 9 Students in Chongqing, China: Determinants of Demand, and Policy Implications. PhD thesis, The University of Hong Kong

Zhang, Wei (2014): 'The Demand for Shadow Education in China: Mainstream Teachers and Power Relations'. *Asia Pacific Journal of Education*, Vol.34, No.4, pp.436–454.

Zhang, Wei (2018): *Juku: Historical Development and Changing Policy Orientation*. Working Paper submitted to Ministry of Education, Beijing. [in Chinese]

Zhang, Wei (2019): 'Regulating Private Tutoring in China: Uniform Policies, Diverse Responses'. *ECNU Review of Education*[East China Normal University], Vol.2, No.1, pp.25–43.

Zhang, Wei (2021a): 'Analysis of Online Surveys before and after Double Reduction on Demand for Tutoring'. Field notes. Centre for International Research in Supplementary Tutoring, East China Normal University, Shanghai.

Zhang, Wei (2021b): 'Modes and Trajectories of Shadow Education in Denmark and China: Fieldwork Reflections by a Comparativist'. *ECNU Review of Education* [East China Normal University], Vol.4, No.3, pp.615–629.

Zhang, Wei & Bray, Mark (2016): 'Shadow Education: The Rise and Implications of Private Supplementary Tutoring', in Guo, Shibao & Guo, Yan (eds.), *Spotlight on China: Changes in Education under China's Market Economy*. Rotterdam: Sense Publishers, pp.85–99.

Zhang, Wei & Bray, Mark (2017): 'Micro-Neoliberalism in China: Public-Private Interactions at the Confluence of Mainstream and Shadow Education'. *Journal of Education Policy*, Vol.32, No.1, pp.63–81.

Zhang, Wei & Bray, Mark (2018): 'Equalising Schooling, Unequalising Private Supplementary Tutoring: Access and Tracking through Shadow Education in China'. *Oxford Review of Education*, Vol.44, No.2, pp.221–238.

Zhang, Wei & Bray, Mark (2020): 'Comparative Research on Shadow Education: Achievements, Challenges, and the Agenda Ahead'. *European Journal of Education*, Vol.55, No.3, pp.322–341.

Zhang, Wei & Bray, Mark (2021): 'A Changing Environment of Urban Education: Historical and Spatial Analysis of Private Supplementary Tutoring in China'. *Environment and Urbanization*, Vol.33, No.1, pp.43–62.

Zhang, Wei & Yamato, Yoko (2018): 'Shadow Education in East Asia: Entrenched but Evolving Private Supplementary Tutoring', in Kennedy, Kerry & Lee, John C.K. (eds.), *Routledge International Handbook on Schools and Schooling in Asia*. London: Routledge, pp.323–332.

Index

advertising 19, 23, 24, 40, 52, 61, 65, 67, 68–70, 73, 74, 79, 82, 114
Africa xvi, 16; Central 110; North 3, 30; sub-Saharan 16, 30
after-school programme 35, 65, 73, 74, 118
Argentina 17, 121
Asia xvii, xviii, 3, 31; East xiv, 1, 15–16; South xiv, 1
Australia 10, 16, 30, 34; Western 23, 34, 35, 103
Australian Tutoring Association 34
Austria 121
Azerbaijan 121

Bahrain 16
Bangladesh 16, 121
Bhutan 31
Brazil 121
Brunei Darussalam 32

Cambodia xviii, 2, 9, 10, 11, 16, 29–30, 31, 122
Canada 10, 122
China v, xv, xvii, xviii, 2, 3, 11, 12, 15, 20, 21, 22–27, 29–31, 33, 58–88, 105, 109, 110, 113, 116–119, 122
contracts 19, 23, 35, 36, 52, 54, 69, 70, 71, 103, 104, 111, 115, 116, 119
corruption 19, 29, 62, 79, 86, 88
COVID-19 11, 29–30, 34, 35, 38–40, 60–62, 66–69, 95, 96, 102, 110, 111, 118, 119

curfews 10, 24, 25, 65, 115
curriculum xiv, 2, 18, 26, 27, 30, 35, 37, 47, 48–52, 54, 60, 63–65, 67, 73, 75, 99, 111, 115, 117, 118
Cyprus 17, 122
Czech Republic 30, 123

Denmark xiv, 2, 3, 20, 23, 38, 97–105, 113, 119, 120
double-reduction policy 70, 72–76, 77
dual-tutor model 7, 60, 110, 116
duration of tutoring 25, 26, 32, 114, 115

Education for All (EFA) 32, 51, 70, 117, 119
educational broadcasting system 35
effectiveness: of policies 12, 37, 39, 74, 109, 111; of tutoring 15, 18, 39, 68, 73, 99; of regulation 8, 66, 69, 83, 93, 105, 110, 113–114
Egypt xiv, 3, 10, 16, 28, 31, 89–96, 99, 110, 113, 118, 120,
equity 2, 3, 17, 34, 36, 39, 50, 51, 70, 72, 109, 117, 119
enactment xv, xvii, xviii, 12, 14, 21, 27, 28, 59, 65, 66, 72, 73, 74, 75, 76, 77, 88, 111, 112, 116,
England 11, 18, 38, 39, 40, 119, 127; England and Wales 11, 127
Eritrea 30
ethics 19, 29, 64, 65; *see also* corruption
Ethiopia 21, 26

Europe xiv, xvii, 3, 16, 97; Eastern 16; Northern 17, 37, 97; Southern 16; Western 16, 97
examination 15, 17, 18, 26, 29, 30, 47, 49, 50, 51, 53, 55, 59, 63, 68, 71, 79, 84, 86, 89, 93–95, 100, 102, 105, 113, 115

fees 23, 26, 27, 35, 56, 62, 65, 66, 69, 70, 74, 76, 82, 91, 94, 114
fire safety 21, 66, 84, 85, 111, 114
France 10
franchise 9, 49

Gambia, The 11, 30
Germany 123
Ghana 10
Greece 16–17, 30, 120

Hong Kong xvii, xviii, 11, 15, 20, 23, 26, 29, 123
hygiene 17, 21, 114

India xv, 3, 16, 79–88, 99, 109, 110, 113, 114
internet 7, 8, 9, 125
Iran 123
Iraq 16, 22, 31

Japan 2, 3, 10, 11, 12, 15, 16, 20, 21, 23, 24, 28, 30, 31, 34, 35–36, 45–57, 87, 88, 101, 111, 112, 113, 116–119, 124
Jordan 16

Kazakhstan 25, 124
Kenya 11, 30, 111, 124
Korea, South [Republic of] xiv, 2, 10, 12, 15, 16, 20–28, 31, 35, 112, 113, 116, 118, 125
Kuwait 16, 31

laissez faire approaches 12, 28, 30, 33, 82, 109
Latin America 17
Lesotho 118

Macao 20
Maharashtra 79, 81, 82, 84

Malaysia 22, 32
Maldives 33
mathematics 7, 45, 50, 63
Mauritius 10, 16, 32, 113, 118, 120, 125
media 14, 68, 70, 74, 77, 100, 111
MentorDanmark 98, 100–103
Mozambique 125
Myanmar xviii, 2, 31, 51

Namibia 118
Nepal 126
Netherlands 38
non-profit organisations (NPOs) 9, 11, 36, 38
Norway xviii, 11

Olympiad 26, 63, 64
Oman 31
online tutoring xiv, 8, 9, 11, 25, 27, 60–69, 71, 77, 87, 99, 100, 102, 105, 110, 111, 116, 122

Pakistan 26, 126
Palestine 31
Poland 126
public-private partnership xv, xviii, 33, 35, 39, 40, 50, 55–57, 60, 118
premises: schools 10, 32, 34, 35, 63, 82; tutoring centres 21, 32, 60, 65, 99, 100, 103, 111
protest 83, 84, 87, 95

Qatar 16, 126

registration 9, 20, 21, 27, 32, 65, 74, 82, 83, 93, 114, 115
Russia 20, 22, 25, 27
Rwanda 33

SACMEQ 110, 124, 125, 127
science 7, 46, 63, 86
self-regulation xv, 9, 12, 14, 52–57, 74–77, 87, 88
Shanghai xvii, xviii, 69, 75, 77, 111
Singapore 32, 126
social class 1, 59, 73, 92
South Africa 110, 127
Sri Lanka 26, 39, 113, 127

152 *Index*

suicide 23, 84, 86
Sustainable Development Goals 2, 3, 109
Sutton Trust 11, 116,
Sweden 11, 37, 100, 103, 119

Taiwan 12, 23, 31
taxation 19, 21, 39, 82, 94, 104, 111, 116
textbooks 50, 54, 73, 94
Thailand 126
Trinidad & Tobago 127
Tunisia 32
Turkey 10, 30

Ukraine 20, 22
UNESCO xvii, xviii, 2, 109, 117, 119
United Arab Emirates 10, 16, 30, 127
USA 2, 10, 11, 29–30, 38, 39–40, 87, 111, 119, 127
Uzbekistan 10, 21, 25, 26, 27, 30

Vietnam 16

World Bank 90, 94, 95

Zambia 30
Zimbabwe 30, 32

For Product Safety Concerns and Information please contact our EU representative GPSR@taylorandfrancis.com
Taylor & Francis Verlag GmbH, Kaufingerstraße 24, 80331 München, Germany

www.ingramcontent.com/pod-product-compliance
Lightning Source LLC
Chambersburg PA
CBHW060349190426
43201CB00043B/1779